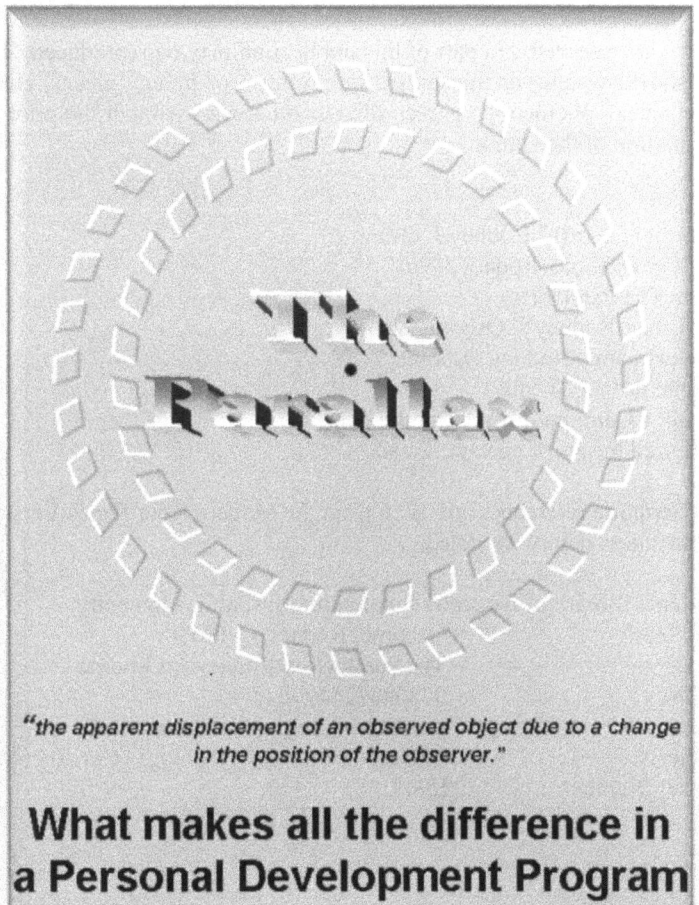

The Parallax

"the apparent displacement of an observed object due to a change in the position of the observer."

What makes all the difference in a Personal Development Program

Rodney J. Osborne

The Parallax

All rights reserved. No part of this publication may be reproduced, stored in a retrieval system, or transmitted in any form or by any means, electronic, mechanical, photocopying, recording or otherwise, without the prior written permission of the author.

Copyright © 2012 Rodney J. Osborne
Author: Osborne, Rodney, 1963
Title: The Parallax
Publisher: Rodney J. Osborne, 2012
Contact name: Rodney Osborne
Phone: 0416 110 280
Email: kasumi.publishing@gmail.com
Preferred means of contact: Email

All Scripture references are taken from the Modern King James Version Bible unless otherwise stated.

National Library of Australia Cataloguing-in-Publication entry
Author: Osborne, Rodney J., 1963-
Title: The Parallax/by Rodney J. Osborne
ISBN: 9780987254900 (pbk)
Notes: Includes bibliographical references.
Subjects: Self-actualisation (Psychology) Christian life.
Dewey Number: 158.1

Printed with the assistance of: www.loveofbooks.com.au

"The formula of success in the world has simply nothing in common with the truth expressed by the Word of God."
(Barnhouse, The invisible war, 1965, pg.222)

"Grace and peace be multiplied to you through the knowledge of God and of Jesus our Lord, according as His divine power has given to us all things that pertain to life and godliness, through the knowledge of Him who has called us to glory and virtue, through which He has given to us exceedingly great and precious promises, so that by these you might be partakers of the divine nature, having escaped the corruption that is in the world through lust. **But also in this very thing, bringing in all diligence, filling out your faith with virtue, and with virtue, knowledge; and with knowledge self-control, and with self-control, patience, and with patience, godliness, and with godliness, brotherly kindness, and with brotherly kindness, love.** For if these things are in you and abound, they make you to be neither idle nor unfruitful in the knowledge of our Lord Jesus Christ."
(2Pe 1:2-8)

Dedication & Acknowledgements

To all Personal Development practitioners, and particularly those who I trained and worked with over the past ten years or so: You helped me see what works and in some cases, what doesn't, as well as how deep, or in some cases, how shallowly Personal Development has reached into our souls.

Also big thanks to my friend, Doug Forrest, for giving me invaluable feedback on how the material in this book reads and how it may be received.

Most of all: expressions of massive gratitude to my daughter, Jenna Osborne. You have been my spelling and grammar checker as well as a sounding board as I spoke, at times, without ceasing about the ideas in this book. Your input and contribution makes you truly a part of the 'family business.'

Warning!

"It is highly dangerous to receive the truth of the Bible with human wisdom, for this is a hidden and subtle method which invariably causes a believer to perfect with his flesh the work of the Holy Spirit."

(The Spiritual Man, Watchman Nee)

Table of Contents

Part 1: Introducing Personal Development 6
  Introduction 6
  The History of Personal Development 14
  Personal Development Theory 29
Part 2: The Principles 35
  Systems, Platforms, Frameworks and Programs 35
  More on God's Personal Development System 54
  Faith 59
  Virtues 63
    Truth-P-Tolerance 65
    Grace-P-Greed 75
    Love-P-Self-centeredness 85
    Servant-hood P Significance 93
    Humility- P- Pride 105
    Justice-P-Oppression 112
    Self Control-P-Sensualism 123
  Knowledge 133
  Self-Control 139
  Patience 143
  Godliness 148
  Brotherly Kindness 158
  Love 164
  Conclusion 171
  The prayer to become a believer 183
  Appendix A - Doctrine of the five cycles of discipline 184

Part 1: Introducing Personal Development

Introduction

'PARALLAX': IT'S AN INTERESTING WORD that describes the purpose of this book. It means:

> *"1. the apparent displacement of an observed object due to a change in the position of the observer. 2. the difference between the view of an object as seen through the picture-taking lens of a camera and the view as seen through a separate viewfinder. 3. an apparent change in the position of cross hairs as viewed through a telescope, when the focusing is imperfect."*[1]

Have you ever been driving along on a clear night and you notice the apparent magnification of the full moon? There it hangs, a perfect circle reflecting the light from the sun and twice as large as normal. It seems to be the size of a basket ball rather than its normal ping-pong ball size. As you drive down the street you turn your gaze to get the attention of a passenger, taking your eyes off the moon for but a moment. "Look at how big the moon is tonight!" you exclaim as you turn back to view this awesome sight. In what seems to be but a moment, the moon has shrunk back to its normal size.

What has happened? An ancient Greek called Ptolemy (pronounced without the 'p') came up with a mathematical

---

[1] Dictionary.com, in *Dictionary* (2010).

system based on the theory that the planets and the sun revolved around the earth. From this system he was able to predict that the moon would sometimes come twice as close to the earth than other times, hence the moon appearing twice the size as normal. His maths is probably correct, but we now know the universe does not revolve around us. I know there are those that think it does, but even the science of today won't back up self-centeredness.

Getting back to our drive in the car, in that brief moment, you drove a small distance and changed your position in respect to the position of the moon. The angle of your view is different and so the moon appears different. It actually hasn't changed size at all. Nor has the observer changed in that moment. Only the position of the observer has changed.

If the reader has had this experience, he has experienced a parallax of perception. This book will, should the reader be open to it, demonstrate many parallax's in the area known these days as Personal Development.

I have spent just over a decade in an occupation that placed the highest priority on Personal Development: reading books and listening to tapes which evolved into CD's and MP3's. To give the reader some idea of my previous commitment to this area, here is what I did over that period:

- Reading a minimum of 20 books a year (cover to cover).
- Listen to 5 CD's/Tapes per week, 52 weeks a year.
- Purchased over 300 Personal Development books. (I stopped counting here)
- Downloaded every free Personal Development book he could find (seems too numerous to count).
- The proud owner of the largest Personal Development library in that organisation at the time.

- Completed book reviews (as a habit) on most of what was read and/or listened to (these reviews came in handy for the planning and preparation of this book).

If the above list is a sign of commitment, I have not found anyone that can match (within the company that I kept) this commitment to the importance of Personal Development.

As an interesting self-observation, I, on the other hand have not been able to match the results in the workplace of those much less committed to Personal Development. The underlying logical message, or assumption, is that a commitment to Personal Development will show itself in the success of results required or sought. What makes my observation interesting is that the assumption didn't work. It did, as the saying goes about assumptions, indeed make 'An ASS out of U and ME. In some ways, this book points out how we can be a bit of an ASS when it comes to the whole field of Personal Development.

The question of 'why did my results not reflect the Personal Development I was doing?' started the idea for this book.

Another curious observation was that I found books that were life changing for me. The personal results were truly outstanding. These books are re-read often, and marked heavily with a highlighter. Most of those others who had a lesser commitment, found these same books, boring and difficult to read and, did not hesitate to inform me accordingly, as though they were an authority on the subject.

They were also 'self-proclaimed' authorities on their own set of favourite books, which were considered prominently as, almost and close to that of Scripture (The Bible, which is one of the books held with little regard or just plain ignored). Interestingly, actual Scripture was not included in their list. I have read or attempted to read these recommended books and found them boring and difficult to read and, to put it bluntly, there is more usefulness to be found for toilet paper. Unlike my contemporaries, I have hesitated to express these thoughts on these 'text-arrhea'[2] excuses for books… up 'til now.

In the end, the majority of my Personal Development books have been consigned to the same section as the 'fiction' part of my library. A good novel, which is enjoyed, is almost believable, but it remains real only in the readers' imagination. And that is why most of the authors of Personal Development books are in the same section as novels.

I am acutely aware and realised that some would be offended, particularly some of those authors, whom I will try not to name or even drop any hints as to their identity. I have no desire to draw any more attention to them. After all, they have committed their own life and considerable resources to their messages, and I actually hold them in high regard for that. Offence though, is a choice, and if their Personal Development works, they would be big enough to (certainly bigger than me) get over it. Whether these people get offended or not, there is at least one thing known. They will not take or be responsible for what takes place in my life if I follow their advice and fail. In some ways, perhaps they shouldn't, but I do believe that there is some responsibility involved when giving advice, especially advise for a life.

I don't see any guarantees to the effect of giving me my money back for the book that led me astray, nor will they fix up the mess, should a mess result. In fact, disclaimers are starting to appear in some of this material. One set of CD's recently (to the time of writing) received basically gave a guarantee that my life would be changed and be magnificently successful as a result of applying the principles contained in this set. And here comes the disclaimer – if it doesn't work it is no fault of the speaker,

---

[2] Text-arrhea: a term I invented to describe the condition of diarrhea, but with words.

but all mine because I must not have followed it perfectly, word for word and exactly.

I got what I deserved with this set of CD's. They were free, designed, to promote the main seminar coming up in the near future. I realised this ploy early and besides the irritating voice that started to sound just like another well known Personal Development speaker, and the remarkable similarities of material to that other speaker, I used my God-given right to choose the stop button on the CD player, and then the eject button.

These speakers will hurry to take all the credit should I be successful as a result of their advice. They take the credit by way of my donations and spending hundreds and sometimes thousands of dollars on their next seminar, as well as doing some marketing for them through word of mouth with my friends.

Make no mistake, my success or failure ultimately is all my responsibility, and so it is with where I place the books in my library.

This book will offend some. It is in places confronting, hard hitting and it is completely biased towards the Bible believing Christian. It will even show favouritism towards 'believers'. No apology will be forthcoming on that. The reader can choose right now whether or not to continue. If the reader doesn't like it, stop reading at the end of this introduction, and put it in your fiction section. I would hasten to add, before you do, consider the stakes of the game you are playing. What if you reach the top of the ladder you are climbing with your life only to discover it was leaning against the wrong wall! Or worse still, not only is it the wrong wall, but it collapses, like that wall in Germany!

This is a book about the real guaranteed Personal Development Program, as well as grave error I made. With more than a decade of studying, reading and trying to follow Personal Development principles, I could even find them in the Bible, but they still didn't work to the satisfaction I expected or to the degree that the Personal Development guru's said they would – and here is why:

> *"Due to the clear division between spirit and soul, outwardly our soul may be disturbed and consequently suffer but inwardly our spirit remains calm and composed as though nothing had happened... Upon arriving at this restful position the believer shall find that all he heretofore had lost for the Lord's sake has today been restored. He has gained God, and therefore everything belonging to God belongs to him as well...his intention is unto God, yet simultaneously he aims at self-glory, self-pleasure, self-comfort. Such a life is a defiled one.* **He walks by faith but also walks by feeling, he follows the spirit but also follows the soul.**"[3]

We are now reading about what the Bible teaches in regard to Personal Development and those that present it. It tells us to test the spirits. The main test is *"any who honours Jesus with less than full Deity expresses the 'spirit of the antichrist'."*[4]

> **"and every spirit that does not confess that Jesus Christ has come in the flesh is not of God. And this is the antichrist you heard is coming, and even now is already in the world." (1Jn 4:3)**

The New Testament book of Jude describes how these teachers secretly slip in amongst us.

> **"For certain men crept in secretly, those having been of old previously written into this condemnation, ungodly ones perverting the grace of our God for**

---

[3] Watchman Nee, *The Spiritual man* (1977).
[4] Lawrence O. Richards, *The Daily Devotional Commentary* (USA: Victor Books, 1990).

unbridled lust, and denying the only Master, God, even our Lord Jesus Christ." (Jud 1:4)

This book will reveal these false teachings for what they are by two identifying marks. The first, they deny Jesus Christ, even in part, making Him out to be less than God. The second, they reject or twist the meaning of grace, which is so fundamental to the Christian faith.

The Personal Development that comes from these false teachers may very well give lifestyle/luxury, achievement and success. It will also ultimately give you dissatisfaction, sadness and unfulfilment.

On the other hand, the Personal Development that comes out of accepting that Jesus Christ is the Son of God and therefore the Creator of all these timeless and infallible principles, coupled with the doctrine of Grace may provide lifestyle/luxury, achievement and success, as well as most assuredly, definitely and guaranteed satisfaction, happiness and fulfilment.

There is a more fundamental question buried deep in here. If by my experience, largely a negative experience, with personal development, why haven't I given up on the whole idea? Many, now critics, have. In fact, I have seen so many leave similar positions and give up on any further personal development. They sell or give away their books and tapes/CD's. As for me, I doubt if I will ever stop developing myself. I think there is a sense of the truth in the quote, *"The only thing necessary for the triumph [of evil] is for good men to do nothing."* (Edmund Burke). Should I stop personal development, it would not be long before I represent a ruin. All I have to do to triumph over this natural decline of my humanity is *"do something!"* (Shihan Stacey Karetsian, GKR Conference 2008).

That 'something' to do is experience a parallax. All it takes is a 'parallax'. A change in your position from an unbeliever to a believer.

Throughout this book a definition of the parallax will appear. I found this necessary whilst writing and it occurred to me that it might be the same for my readers. Dr Cloud said it well; *"Humans tend to be unable to hold opposite ideas in dynamic tension. But this tension we will always need to hold.*[5]

> *Parallax: "the apparent displacement of an observed object due to a change in the position of the observer."*

Note on quotes used in this book

This book contains a large number of quotes which fit into one of two categories:

Source documents: these quotes have come from books and documents that I personally have and have been referenced accordingly. I have endeavoured to use these quotes within context and to reflect the meaning intended by the authors.

Secondary documents: These are quotes of quotes which may or may not have come from a source document not in my possession. There are many dangers in using secondary documents in regard to correct quoting, context, and referencing. Some are taken from web sites and accuracy, context and referencing can be doubtful. Judgements made on the authors of these quotes should be made with care, or not made at all until the source has been validated.

It would be considered a valid question as to why I would use quotes from secondary documents in this book. I have included such quotes because they help make my point. They are not a reflection on the source or secondary author in any way.

---

[5] Dr John Townsend Dr. Henry Cloud, *How People Grow* (Sydney: Strand Publishing, 2001). 113.

The History of Personal Development

"We learn from history that we never learn anything from history." (Hegel)

"History teaches everything, even the future." (Alphonse de Lamartine)

"No one can hope to write history without presuppositions... Back of the selection is a conviction of what is important."[6]

WHAT WE LEARN IS A CHOICE and because we don't make that choice, we don't learn especially from history. There is but one human history with innumerable ways of looking at it. Here we are looking at the history from the perspective of the field of 'Personal Development'. It is about the growth, maturation, and the gaining of wisdom of mankind with the purpose of the development of the human condition. It is something that goes back as far as the Garden of Eden where man fell short of God by one act of disobedience.

The main lesson to learn, in the context of this book, from the history of Personal Development is that once mankind tries to remove God from the picture, or his efforts, the full power of any Personal Development principle or practice is limited or even nullified, and some false ineffective ones are invented.

Instead of starting from the Garden, let's begin with the some more recent teaching and then work backwards through time. Stephen Covey in his 2004 edition of 'The 7 Habits of Highly Effective People' comments on his own study of success literature, *"...much of the success literature of the past 50 years was superficial."*[7]. Just three pages later he writes, *"I found that the things I was teaching and knew to be effective were often at variance with these popular voices."*[8]. I personally have found that the Personal Development or success literature that I

---

[6] Latourette, *A History of Christianity* (Harper, 1975).
[7] Stephen R. Covey, *The 7 Habits of Highly Effective People* (2004).
[8] Ibid.

studied, which included some of the most highly recommended titles in the world, and tried to apply were working, but only to a frustratingly low level of effectiveness. These are the popular voices and they are missing something. Covey goes on to point out that all the success literature over the past 200 years can be grouped into two ethic groups.

One is the Character ethic. It teaches that *"there are basic principles of effective living, and that people can only experience true success and enduring happiness as they learn and integrate these principles into their basic character."*[9]

Principles of effective living might include integrity, humility, fidelity, temperance, courage, justice, patience, and so on. They all sound great, and no doubt are great. They are also all mentioned in the Bible as desirable character traits. For many of those 'popular voices' who also have no hesitation in denying God or the direct naming of Him, all these principles become corrupted like a worm virus in their souls computer.

The other group is the personality ethic. This one teaches that *"Success became more a function of personality, of public image, of attitudes and behaviours, skills and techniques..."*[10] This ethic takes two paths – a] human and public relations techniques, and b] Positive Mental Attitude. Those that follow this group have that 'charismatic' personality and have great technique for influencing others. The problem is if you have another type of personality, perhaps that of an introvert, you will never be successful. The personality ethic also comes crashing down as people realise that a 'technique' is being used on them and with the feeling of being conned or sold, walk away. The practitioner of this may answer by saying, 'others won't see what they are doing.' That may be the case, but for fewer and fewer. We are getting smarter and every day this

---

[9] Ibid.
[10] Ibid.

game is over for more and more. In fact, it doesn't even take that; *"it simply makes no difference how good the rhetoric is or even how good the intentions are; if there is little or no trust, there is no foundation for permanent success."*[11]

There is nothing necessarily morally wrong with both the Character and Personality Ethic, until, that is, they are utilised by a person. The two ethics are merely a stage for which the internal principles and values of the person to be played out or expressed. The thief with a great personality ethic will be good at swindling others. A home intruder may wait patiently (a character ethic trait) for the occupants to go out before he breaks in and robs the house. It is the fundamental beliefs and values of each person that determines the morality of the ethic.

An examination of much of the Personal Development literature out there has information and trains of thoughts that if traced back exposes either the outright denial of God or a strong belief in the theory of evolution, or some obscure comment about all gods being the same thing, like a force. This has its roots in the Darwinian revolution.

Before we commence a brief and general look at the history of Personal Development, a note about my approach is needed. I will look at history going backwards. In other words starting with present day and moving back in time in chunks, marked by what I see as significant events that highlight the thread of God's inclusion, or exclusion in the passage of Personal Development.

History is not one of my best or favourite topics and the use of pictures that give an overview are helpful to me. Looking at the History of Personal Development in this way is like looking at the Nile Delta. It begins from one source – the Nile, flowing from south to north into the Delta, and starts to spread, carving out the landscape, branching out into numerous distributaries.

---

[11] Ibid.

By the time we have reached the Mediterranean Sea there are many outlets.

The more I look at the history of Personal Development in this way, the more interesting analogies I find. For example, in the tracing of God in these various and numerable distributaries I find a large population of some of the biggest crocodiles in the world living in these waters. Most know some of the dangers of swimming in these places and the hunting capabilities of these fierce predators. In the same way, adopting some philosophies as a means of Personal Development may be found to be full of crocs.

I also find myself realising that all the distributaries, coming from the same source, are all part of the water from the Nile, or, have an element of Truth. They may be watered down to various degrees or polluted by various soil types or by the way mankind has used it through irrigation. This makes it challenging to locate the truth and one must always return to the source to sample the pure waters.

The diagram below provides a 'satellite' view of how I will approach the history of Personal Development.

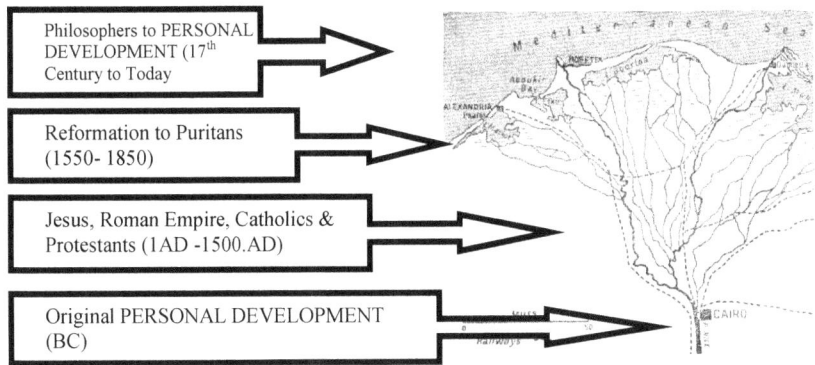

Figure 1. www.probertencyclopedia.com

Philosophers to Personal Development Today

This period begins towards the end of the 'age of enlightenment' through to a present day. Some of the names and events that formed this part of history include Charles Wesley, George Whitefield, Voltaire, and the French revolution, Benjamin Franklin, Alexander Pope, Descartes, Isaac Newton and Charles Darwin. To avoid too much detail, I will confine myself to brief comments on the influence these people and events have on Personal Development today. In no particular order:

Hugo Grotius: (a devout Hollander of the 17th Century) 'de-Christianised' natural law by treating it as an ethic valid *"even if there were no God (which God forbid)."*[12] Even today it is not too hard to find this strain of thought. Natural law works, even if we don't believe there is a God. Consider this: it only works because God created it.

Benjamin Franklin: Proposed that they (the founding fathers of America) pray when the Constitutional Convention was deadlocked. This proposal was rejected because the founding fathers *'felt that politics lies within the domain of man's natural reason, which should not be abdicated.'*[13] Here we see the effects of the Deists idea of where God belongs in the matters of mankind. In a word, it's called pride, or another word: independence. Man is seen to be clever enough to take care of himself and he doesn't need God.

Deism: A religion where God has done such a great job of creation that He can now withdraw from involvement and leave man to order their own affairs.

Voltaire and the French Revolution: seen as the prophet of the French deist's, making a significant contribution to the French

---

[12] Ronald H. Bainton, *A History of Christianity* (London: Thomas Nelson & Sons, 1964).
[13] Ibid.

revolution. This ushered in what is known as the age of progress (1789-1914), Bastille Day (14th July 1789) marks the beginning of the celebration of, *"the democratic gospel of the French revolution rested upon the glorification of man rather than God."*[14] Much of today's Personal Development promotes how good mankind is at developing themselves.

<u>Alexander Pope</u>: in the end had to admit that man is unable to find an explanation.

<u>Descartes</u>: thought, he *"ought to begin with an attitude of universal doubt."*[15] In other words, he disbelieved everything until it was proven. Though we might call that negative thinking today, many still think this way.

<u>Darwinian revolution</u> is the effect of the theory of evolution proposed in 1858 by Charles Darwin and Alfred Wallace. The theory of evolution says that there are changes *'over time in one or more inherited traits found in populations of organisms.'*

These changes amongst other areas include behavioural characteristics that change as a result of gene/environment interactions. There are two processes that could be involved: a] natural selection (survival of the fittest), or b] genetic drift (random changes). The theory of evolution has impacted nearly every field within biology as well as non-biology areas and disciplines like agriculture, anthropology, philosophy and psychology.

It is claimed that there is no belief in God required for this theory to work. Evolution is merely the next step from the Newtonian Revolution

---

[14] Bruce L. Shelley, *Church History in Plain English* (Thomas Nelson, 1975).
[15] Justo L. Gonzalez, *The Story of Christianity, Volume 2, The Reformation to the Present day*, vol. 2 (New York: HarperCollins, 2010).

Newtonian Revolution is the age that said, *"What God did was put in place a universe with certain principles, and what we need to do is figure out how those principles work."*[16].

God no longer makes decisions. He set things in place to happen automatically and withdrew. From this we can conclude that we don't need God anymore. We need only to learn how to work with the principles.

Prior to this age there was virtually no room for the promotion of Personal Development because of the fundamental belief that God simply makes all decisions.

Wesley, Whitefield & Edwards: these were revivalist, preaching the Word of God in England and America. Wesley's preaching style was intellectual and doctrinal. Whitefield's style was dramatic and emotional. Jonathon Edwards lacked in being a 'good public speaker' but he made up for it with the potent sermon he is famous for: 'Sinners in the hands of an angry God.' If we were able to put these three styles into one Personal Development speaker, I have to wonder what impact would follow. More critical to note here is that the thread of God in the delivery of Personal Development was not restricted by the style of delivery.

From a bird's eye perspective on where Personal Development is happening at this point in history, it's not hard to exclaim, 'What a mess!' What a mixture. A mixture of Deism (Europe & English colonies), Revivalists (Wesley, Whitefield), Pietism (Germany and Scandinavia), The Great Awakening (Jonathon Edwards in America), and the Rationalists (all the other philosophers of the day) making their contributions. It is beginning to look like the Nile Delta at its most northern parts. There are so many distributaries and channels, that it can get confusing as to which one to follow. Some follow a mixture of

---

[16] Jerry I. Porras Jim Collins, *Built to Last* (New York: HarperCollins House, 1994). 41.

many. Perhaps by identifying some, we at least know where some of our own personal philosophy comes from. The thread of where God is in all this is picking up on the where Wesley, Whitefield, Edwards and the like came from, which interestingly is the same place all the others came from. Let's move south where the Delta begins to thin out.

Reformation to Puritans

The puritans – a title coined in the 1560s describes a much misunderstood group which formed much of the 'Protestant religion.' Back then and to some degree today, they are seen as a *'odd, furious, and ugly form of Protestant religion.'*[17] For those who have looked into it, they were *'sober, conscientious, and cultured citizens, persons of principle, devoted, determined, and disciplined, excelling in the domestic virtues, and with no obvious shortcomings save a tendency to run to words when saying anything important, whether to God or to man.'*[18] These people were visionaries, passionate, goal orientated, practical and methodical. They got all this from their understanding of the Bible. Mostly, the Puritans were the Pilgrims that settled in the now named USA.

The reformation – The Puritans were a product of what is known as the Reformation. There is a great deal already written about this time in history, which commenced around the time of King Henry VIII. It is my intention to take out of the massive pile of information, one point. That is that of one of the most significant events to take place: The printing and publishing of the Bible. Many of my readers would have heard of the King James Version. As people started to read the Bible for themselves, groups with various interpretations of how to live were formed. One of which was the Puritans. Previous to this, the scriptures were closely guarded and written in an ancient

---

[17] James I. Packer, "Why we need the Puritans," (1996).
[18] Ibid.

language that only the qualified Roman Catholic priest could read or even have access to. I might remind the reader that this is an over-simplification of what took place and by whom, and I do this only to keep us focused on the theme of this book.

The majority opinion of this time was that man had no power or ability to change anything that happened. If a crop failed, it was an act of God. If someone died, it was God's will. With God being all responsible and man just a cog in the works, there was no motivation to even consider improving or taking control and responsibility for one's life.

The future is in the hands of God, *"...the Christian will say. True, but that must not be said in the interests of escaping the responsibility of trying to influence that future for good. God works through human instrumentality."*[19]

Just because there was little to none, what we would call Personal Development, at the time; this does not mean that it started at the end of this age. Personal Development has actually been around since the beginning of Bible times.

The introduction of the Roman Catholic Church takes us further south in our 'Delta' view of Personal Development history.

Jesus to the Roman Empire

The Roman Empire – When an empire as great as the Roman Empire collapses, much of its influences remains. One of those influences, and again I am aware of the over-simplification, was the Roman Catholic Church and the Pope. The first Pope, according to church was Saint Peter, the disciple of Jesus Christ of Nazareth. This is my understanding from a Protestant who doesn't claim to be anywhere close to an expert on the Catholic church, so I am open to correction if I get some of the detail (I

---

[19] John M. L. Young, *The Two Empires in Japan* (Tokyo: The Bible Times Press, 1958). 221-22.

am deliberately avoiding) incorrect. We are merely tracing the thread of where God is in the history of Personal Development.

This brings us to Jesus Christ and the times that he was living in. Street teachers were in abundance during this time and three books in the New Testament (2 Peter, 2 Timothy and Jude) identify and warn the church of 'false teachers'. From these records, we can see that these street teachers sought to attract adherents by giving lectures on how to live, solve problems, and find meaning to life. It doesn't sound too different than what we have today. We call them motivational speakers or something like that. Today the platform is far greater. There are live seminars, seminars conducted on the internet, books and recordings of seminars or teaching.

On Jesus, *'He was but one of a large number of itinerant teachers who shared their insight into life and its meaning,...'*[20] I made a note here that we don't know very much about any of the others. It seems, only Jesus has stood the ultimate test of time. He has had such an impact, we still count our years by His time BC = before Christ. AD = anno Domini.

The original Personal Development

The original Personal Development is traced back to the Hebrew Scriptures. Even Philo of Alexandria (20BC-AD40), a contemporary of Jesus, claimed that *"since the Hebrew prophets antedated the Greek philosophers, the latter must have drawn from the wisdom of the former."*[21] In other words, he said *"whatever was true in the philosophy of the Greeks had been said earlier by Jewish scripture."*[22]

---

[20] John Drane, *Introducing the New Testament*, third ed. (Oxford: A Lion Book, 2010).
[21] Justo L. Gonzalez, *The Story of Christianity*, vol. 1, The Early Church to the Dawn of the Reformation (New York: Harper Collins, 2010). 19.
[22] Harry R. Boer, *A short History of the Early Church* (Grand Rapids, Michigan: William B. eerdmans, 1976).

About 500 to 600 years before Philo was Ephesus. He developed the thought of 'one can never step into the same water twice.' I seem to recall another more recent 'Guru' saying the same thing. Also there was an ancient philosopher called Heraclitus. He came out with this 'new age' thought, 'all things flow.' Perhaps it's not so new after all.

We can see from historical records that philosophers such a Plato and Socrates, *"and many other philosophers had criticized the ancient gods and had taught about a supreme being, perfect and immutable"*[23], revealing they had been influenced by the supreme, perfect and immutable God described in the Hebrew scriptures. Socrates (450BC) was different from many previous philosophers because he was more interested in the quality of men then the nature of the world. The 'quality of men' is a 450BC way of saying personal development.

There were other philosophies developing around this period such as the 'Stoics' founded by Zeno (335-263BC). *"Ancient philosophers often searched for a single principle that lay at the heart of all things, and for the Stoics that core property was 'reason'."*[24] They had such high personal and moral standards that it was not uncommon to commit suicide rather than lose self-respect or dignity. The Stoics *"believed that the purpose of philosophy was to understand the law of nature, and to obey and adjust to it. The wise person is not one who knows a great deal, but rather one whose mind is so attuned to the universal law that reason prevails."*[25] Does this sound familiar to some of what we hear today?

---

[23] Gonzalez, *The Story of Christianity*, 1: 22.
[24] Drane, *Introducing the New Testament*: 19.
[25] Gonzalez, *The Story of Christianity*, 1: 23.

There were also the Epicureans. Their core property was 'pleasure'. There were also Gnostics, mystery religions, Judaism and the introduction of Christianity.

It is at this point where Personal Development started to go wrong. There is no doubt that Personal Development started with God as the creator of all the principles required to live a successful life. This can be traced through the Old Testament from which Judaism finds its roots. Many of the street teachers from the Bible times emerged as *"men treated the faith as a 'philosophy."*[26] In doing so, they twisted the truth here and there and ended up with a message that was antagonistic towards the original Personal Development teaching, which in a word is 'godliness.'

> *Parallax: "the apparent displacement of an observed object due to a change in the position of the observer."*

True to form, the Bible gives us the answers and how to identify these 'false teachers'. In the same way, we can use these same answers to judge today whose Personal Development is truth and whose is not. Here is the 'acid test':

1. <u>Denial of the sovereign Lord:</u> Some will do this outright. They will openly state that they believe there is no God. Their honesty is appreciated and I am grateful for letting me know up front that I should not listen to them. Others will attribute what they teach to a 'greater power' that might be a god. It is just a fancier way of denying God. Even more subtle is avoiding the subject altogether but claiming originality to what they teach. There is a very popular motivational speaker around at the time of writing that keeps referring to his 'new technologies' as something he has developed. However, before I heard him, I had read the books he had taken these 'new technologies' from. Again,

---

[26] Richards, *The Daily Devotional Commentary*.

it's just a fancier way of denying God. Taking ownership means denying the Originator of ownership. We call that stealing or plagerism.

2. <u>Produces shameful ways.</u> The question here is what is the fruit? If a teacher obviously has great success, we consider them worth listening to and following. Look a little deeper and you may find the success they have has cost them in areas you may not be willing to pay in. Perhaps they cannot hold a relationship together. Perhaps they have plenty of money, but no happiness. There are an abundance of examples out there in both the church and the Personal Development circuit.

3. <u>Greed.</u> Are they in it for the money? If they are, you can tell because they now have a lot of what was yours. If there is 'no money' in the next seminar, they won't do it. Money becomes the dominant factor in their decision making. It is not that there is anything wrong with making money from Personal Development. It's more about the motive and exploitation.

The Bible makes significant mention of 'false teachers' perhaps because as Robert Penn Warren writes, *"the past is always a rebuke to the present."* He further says, *"History cannot give us a program for the future, but it can give us a fuller understanding of ourselves, and of our common humanity, so that we can better face the future."* We can learn from this brief history of Personal Development. While I don't believe the first half of this quote, the second half rings true: *"History may defeat the Christ but it nevertheless points to him as the law of life."* (Reinhold Niebuhr)

Going back to the beginning of this chapter, we were looking at Covey's comments on the Character ethic. If our core beliefs can be likened to a map, having the right map makes the character ethic important and valid. Likewise, if we have the right map, it makes the personality ethic contribute to a real difference when we are faced with obstacles and frustrations. Covey writes, *"But the first and most important requirement is the accuracy of the map."*[27]

The point of this whole chapter is to say that the right map is primarily the Bible, treated as the Word of God. This book will go on to identify and examine many of the Personal Development principles out there today and show how a parallax[28] has taken place. Keep in mind that God does not change, nor is He the one that has moved. We are the ones that have changed position and therefore see things differently. It is time that we learnt from history and moved back into the position we were originally created to be in.

Another way of looking at the history of Personal Development

On the next page is a timeline/chart which shows three main streams of belief systems. These three systems are broad, including many facets or variations. As an exercise, plot on the chart where you think the people identified fit. Feel free to add anyone I haven't identified. Please note that your choice may not be the same as theirs. This is a personal exercise with neither a right nor wrong answer. After this step, plot where you believe you are on the chart.

We will do this exercise at the end of the book, just to see if there are any changes.

---

[27] Covey, *The 7 Habits of Highly Effective People.*
[28] *"the apparent displacement of an observed object due to a change in the position of the observer."*

PD Time-line/Chart

God's plan for mankind

Western Civilization Shaping Systems

Dogmatic Faith: institutional forms of religion (Catholics, Protestants, Latter day Saints, Jehovah's Witnesses, Islam)

Magus: the cosmos, created by God (or gods) has embedded within divine codes or secrets that reveal ultimate mysteries and knowledge. New Spirituality. Eastern Mysticism [Hindu, Buddhist, Taoist]. Occult [astrology, fortune telling, spiritual guides], reincarnation, karma.)

Rationality: primary truth is knowable through the mind without the need of revelation. (Human Potential, PMA, mind power, Evolution, philosophy, psychology, NLP, Motivational techniques)

Beginning to 1000 BC		Jesus, Roman empire, early church (1ad—1500ad)	Reformation to today (1550—2012 +)	
	1000 BC to 1AD	2AD to 1550	1551 to 2012	2013 to end

Where would you place these people on this chart? Anthony Robbins, Jim Rohn, Steven Covey, Deepak Chopra, Louise Hay, Dr Phil, Edward De Bono, Rodney Osborne.
Where would you place yourself? Plot yourself on the chart now and then again at the end of this book.

Personal Development Theory

THIS CHAPTER IS REALLY ABOUT WHY there has always been a drive in mankind to improve. Covey points to it in his new forward in The 7 Habits of Highly Effective People, where he writes, *"...recognize that **the source** of our basic need for meaning and of the positive things we seek in life is principles – which natural laws I personally believe have their **source in God**."*[29] *(Bold is mine)*

These basic needs were not part of the original man – Adam; until he experienced what we call the 'fall of man' had no such needs. As a result of the fall, mankind is now operating 'out of synch' with the principles that govern how this universe works. As we are made in the likeness of God, there is a constant orientation, or pull, towards getting back to that original state where we function in harmony with those 'God sourced principles.'

To be successful in such a quest would mean no further need of God, or a belief in Him. Perhaps this is one of the reasons God placed two armed angels at the entrance of the Garden, preventing man from re-entering. That doesn't seem to stop us trying though, and many have jumped the gun and excluded God before arriving at the place of perfect harmony. John Maxwell writes, *"When it comes to believing in themselves, some people are agnostic*[30]*. That's not only a shame; it also keeps them from becoming what they could be."*[31]

We all have a drive within us, regardless of degree, that seeks to improve ourselves. There seems to be no end to the methods we can think-up to do so and it all comes out of 'falling short of the

---

[29] Covey, *The 7 Habits of Highly Effective People*.
[30] Agnostic: a person who believes it is impossible to know that God exists
[31] John C Maxwell, *Talent is never enough* (Nashville: Thomas Nelson, 2007).

mark' or a coming up short of the potential we instinctively know we have. This short-fall brings to the surface a set of needs or challenges that we, the human race face.

The challenges that most of us face as a result of this disharmony are *(source of this list is from 'The 7 Habits of Highly Effective Habits', Stephen R. Covey):*

1. <u>Fear and Insecurity</u>: this vulnerability often fosters a resignation to riskless living and to co-dependency.

2. <u>I want it now</u>: we must constantly re-educate and reinvent ourselves, competition is fierce. Sustainability and growth are not considered in this challenge.

3. <u>Blame and victim-ism</u>: If only... if only... if only. Those with this challenge do not possess the humility to accept and take responsibility, nor the courage to take whatever initiative.

4. <u>Hopelessness</u>: Please, would someone just tell me what to do...

5. <u>Lack of life balance</u>: These are always exhausted, in the thick of thin things. They wish for balance and peace of mind, which follows the person who develops a clear sense of his or her highest priorities and who lives with focus and integrity toward them.

6. <u>What's in it for me</u>: Life is a game, a race... Masters in the art of 'Me' instead of the art of 'We'.

7. <u>Hunger to be understood</u>: They feel misunderstood because they feel as though they have little to no influence. The principle of influence is governed by mutual understanding born of the commitment of at least one person to deep listening first.

8. <u>Conflict and differences</u>: Every interaction with others has to be one of conflict. This person feels as though everything

has to be fought for. If it's worth having, you must fight for it.

All of these challenges are found in a humorous story I came across.

A great warship was cautiously sailing down along the coast when a thick fog set in, making visibility extremely poor. The captain of this ship saw the approaching light of another ship, and sent a telegraph message to her, "this is the captain, we are on a collision course. Change your course." A message came back promptly, "change your course." Somewhat annoyed, the captain responded with, "I am the captain of a great warship, change your course." The response, "I don't care, change your course." Now infuriated and beside himself with concern of an impending collision, the captain sends another message, "I am the captain of a very big and great warship and if you do not change your course, I will open fire on you and blow you out of the water. Change your course immediately." There was a pause for a few moments and no change in the now fast approaching light, and then a response, "I am a lighthouse, change course." The captain changed course with no further communication.

Principles are like a lighthouse. They are there to guide, especially through perilous times. Ignore their warning and you will become shipwrecked. If for a moment we are to call principles laws, Covey writes, *"It is impossible for us to break the law. We can only break ourselves against the law"* It doesn't really matter how big and powerful you are, or how eloquent in winning arguments you might be, if you take on these principles by ignoring the Light of the World, a shipwrecked life is all that awaits you.

To summarise the theory of Personal Development, with the use of a parallax, we could say;

- That mankind is born in a condition that misses the goal of full development and perfection. Christians refer to this as 'the sinful man' or 'the unregenerate man.'

- Knowledge of this fallen state creates an internal demand or drive to improve and develop ones-self, leading us to find ways of getting back to that place of being fully developed. One of the most profound lessons in life is as Covey states, *"if you want to achieve your highest aspirations and overcome your greatest challenges, identify and apply the principle or natural law that governs the results you seek."*[32] In The language used by the Christian, this is the 'mans search for God.'

  > **Parallax:** *"the apparent displacement of an observed object due to a change in the position of the observer."*

- Finding and applying these principles to our lives results in self-improvement and development. The Christian calls this being saved. The God factor is vital. Again Covey points to this;

"...one of the basic flaws of the Personality Ethic. To try to change outward attitudes and behaviours does very little good in the long run if we fail to examine the basic paradigms from which those attitudes and behaviours flow."

The basic paradigm is that, 'in the beginning, God.' It is God's will for us to develop to our full potential and gain all the personal success possible and He knows the way. Man without God thinks he knows the way and does so by mimicking God's ways, so of course it works, but only in a limited capacity.

At the risk of being repetitive, Maxwell writes:

---

[32] Covey, *The 7 Habits of Highly Effective People.*

> *"When it comes to believing in themselves, some people are agnostic. That's not only a shame; it also keeps them from becoming what they could be."*[33]

The next section of this book is divided into seven principles of Personal Development taken from 2 Peter 1:3-8. There is an important introduction to this section titled, 'Systems, Frameworks and Platforms. Don't skip this chapter or your understanding of the following principles will be limited. Another note requiring a brief explanation is the wording of headings in the chapter on Virtue. The titles are two words with a 'P' separating them. The 'P' is a symbol meaning parallax: *"the apparent displacement of an observed object due to a change in the position of the observer."*

The first chapter Truth-P-Tolerance reads 'Truth – Parallax – Tolerance.' The chapter will then discuss a group of Personal Development principles and how they will be perceived by the observer, depending on their position. The position taken is not meant to be opposites. The separator is the difference between a 'virtue[34]' (on the left) and a 'value[35]' (on the right).

As you read each chapter, an awareness of a need to change may arise, so for practical purposes, I have included a way to make the changes in order to promote personal growth.

Before we examine these principles of Personal Development, there is an underlying message. Jesus Christ came to re-establish the virtues of God's creation, which on close investigation, are radically different from the values of this world.

There will be many quotes that the Personal Development practitioner will recognise as well as sentences designed to make the reader pause and consider. Here is one:

---

[33] Maxwell, *Talent is never enough*.
[34] Moral goodness, positive moral quality
[35] Importance, usefulness, moral principles, worth

"if we take care of our character (the location of virtue), our reputation (the location of values) will take care of itself."[36] *(Brackets mine)*

---

[36] Dennis Fisher, "What are you Known For?," *Our daily Bread*, no. June, July, August 2011 (2011).

Part 2: The Principles

Systems, Platforms, Frameworks and Programs

BEFORE WE PLUNGE INTO THE MYRIAD of Personal Development principles with their numerous variations of titles, it may be beneficial to get a 'birds eye' view, or a parallax of the systems, frameworks and platforms of the whole subject. What follows in this chapter is a brief summary of my idea of the system, framework and platforms of Personal Development.

To apply Personal Development principles we can firstly see them as part of a system. I will be using Peter Senge's book, 'The Fifth Discipline'[37] as my main source. Then the following author's works will be glanced at to consider the frameworks: Jim Collins and Jerry I Porras[38], Dr Phillip C. McGraw[39], Stephen R. Covey[40]. Then we can consider the platform, or foundation from which to build a framework on; God the Father in the Bible.

There may be some questions from other Personal Development practitioners as to why their favourite author is not included. There are several reasons for this but first; I realise my choice is really a matter of personal preference, drawn from my own extensive reading and study.

---

[37] Peter M. Senge, *The Fifth Discipline* (Australia: Random House, 1990).
[38] Jim Collins, *Built to Last*; Jim Collins, *Good to Great* (New York: HarperCollins House, 2001).
[39] Dr Phillip c McGraw, *Life Strategies* (United Kingdom: Vermillion, 1999).
[40] Covey, *The 7 Habits of Highly Effective People*; Stephen R Covey, *The 8th Habit* (New York: Free Press, 2004).

The first reason is simply a matter of space. I have set a goal for the length of this book and a time to complete it. To include everyone would result in something that looked like a double sized set of multiple volume, 500 page books. I doubt if even the most astute student would find it readable.

Another reason for my choice in authors is these have something I perceive as having a 'sense of truth', in what they write. This is not to say that every other author is lacking truth, even though I could point out a few false teachers. These are just some of the ones I have identified so far. Going back to the beginning of this book, I expressed some perplexity as to why some books, held as great, had no attraction to me while other books, such as these ones, I hold in great esteem while others have difficulty in reading them. I have found the answer that clears up that perplexity and will share this later, but first the foundation for reaching such a conclusion must be established for it to mean anything.

The last reason, which I have saved for last is, some fit into the category of 'Tosser's'[41] These writers have caused enough environmental damage by printing thousands of books by such a degree that to even mention them would further pollute our environment and our minds.

The System

A system is *"the development of methodological thought which proceeds according to the rules of logic and uses methods in order to deal with experiences."*[42]

---

[41] Tosser: an Australian derogatory term describing someone who throws garbage, rubbish or waste products anywhere but the appropriate waste disposal unit. Another offensive name is 'litter bug'.
[42] Paul Tillich, *A History of Christian Thought* (New York: A Touchstone Book, Simon and Schuster, 1967, 1968). xxxvii.

In reality all systems fit into one of two categories; the Divine System, and the worlds system. That statement falls short and does not articulate all that I mean. There is one original System (Divine) and then there are multiple copies of parts of that system (Worlds). The Divine System is created by the Creator.

"He has also settled them forever and ever; He has made a decree which shall not pass away." (Psa 148:6)

The world system is created by the creation. The world system, in many respects, looks a lot like the Divine System because it is but a partial copy. The Bible uses stronger language: *"For they changed the truth of God into a lie, and they worshiped and served the created thing more than the Creator, who is blessed forever. Amen."* (Rom 1:25).

> *Parallax: "the apparent displacement of an observed object due to a change in the position of the observer."*

The Bible also says *"You have wearied Jehovah with your words. Yet you say, In what have we wearied Him? When you say, Every evildoer is good in the eyes of Jehovah, and He delights in them; or, Where is the God of justice?"* (Mal 2:17)

Awareness of systems is important. *"Structures of which we are unaware hold us prisoner."*[43]

As an eighteen year old, I had little, if any, understanding of the oceans currents and behaviours, and being unaware immediately made me a prisoner when I got caught in a rip just off a beach in Newcastle, NSW. I nearly drowned as a result of trying to fight this system of nature. The more I fought it, the harder it fought back. *"The harder you push, the harder the system pushes back."*[44] I have learnt from this near death experience that it is better to go with 'the System' than to fight

---

[43] Senge, *The Fifth Discipline*: 94.
[44] Ibid., 58.

it. The other lesson was to be more careful and swim between the flags.

The rip is part of a system of currents and tides, but that is not the system. The currents and tides are part of the gravitational pulls of earth and the moon. But that is not the system either. The rotation of earth and the orbiting of the moon which all, including the other planets of our solar system that rotate around the sun, absorbs those smaller parts of the system. Our solar system is not the System either, because we know there is a universe. On and on it goes until we conclude that there is a 'natural system' that governs the universe. It all works just fine until I try and create something foreign to the system, like swimming in dangerous waters, as if I can!

There is another lesson here. The more we know of the System, the more integration we can experience working with the System, the more freedom we experience within the disciplines of the System.

There is a parallax, even in systems thinking. *"Now a system is not something in which to dwell. Everybody who dwells within a system feels after some time that it becomes a prison... nevertheless, the system is necessary because it is the form of consistency... So a system cannot be avoided unless you choose to make nonsensical or self-contradictory statements."*[45] Not only can a system become a prison, it can take the 'system dweller' to a place *"above the reality it is supposed to describe."*[46] In other words, to live in and according to a system can cause you to lose your grip on reality. Here the right system becomes important.

Also, keep in mind and consider the potential consequences of taking out the Creators role or existence, on the effective functioning of the System. It's a bit like saying I will run my

---

[45] Tillich, *A History of Christian Thought*: xxxvii.
[46] Ibid.

Mazda 121 on water, because I don't like the cost of fuel. In order for this to work, I would need to change the system. My current internal combustion engine only works on petroleum (unleaded to be precise). We may have several choices of systems for motor vehicles, but once you choose, you cannot violate that system.

My older brother tried it once. When in Japan, he was sent out to wash a fellow-missionaries car. He thought he would go the extra mile and fill up the tank too, with water.

It might be helpful at this point to describe a system by identifying some of its characteristics.

System characteristics

<u>Systems are alive</u>. Not in the sense that humans have life. *"Dividing an elephant in half does not produce two small elephants... living systems have integrity. Their character depends on the whole."*[47] Try to dissect or use just part of a system, and the integrity is lost resulting in operational failure.

<u>Systems require a discipline</u>. *"Systems thinking is a discipline for seeing wholes. It is a framework for seeing interrelationships rather than things, for seeing patterns of change rather than static 'snapshots'."*[48] Disciplines are restraining devices or put another way, controls. A system cannot function if it is allowed to 'free-wheel' out of control. Discipline is an integral part of any system and that is why discipline is so important in people's lives.

To see 'wholes' is to realize *"small changes can produce big results."*[49] Any input into the system grows and has a multiplying effect. *"Cause and effect are not closely related in*

---

[47] Senge, *The Fifth Discipline*: 66.
[48] Ibid., 68.
[49] Ibid., 63.

time and space..."⁵⁰ This is descriptive of how knowledge of a system provides leverage, leverage for limitless efficiency and effectiveness.

Covey, in his book 'The 8ᵗʰ Habit' comments on systems. *"Systems will override rhetoric every day of the week."*⁵¹ In other words: *"When trustworthy people work within structures and systems that are not aligned with the organization's espoused values, the untrustworthy systems will dominate every time."*⁵² Let me reword this for our context; 'the system is the deciding factor of the persons results.' That might be worth chewing on for awhile, especially when the system is the world's system, faulty or insufficient, the operators results will also be faulty or insufficient no matter how good or competent that person is. Later, Covey writes:

> *"Fundamentally, the power is in the System,... the system is stronger than the individual weaknesses of the participants...Marriott Corporation teaches that the devil lies in the details, but success lies in the system."*⁵³

From this it's not too hard to deduce that we all operate in a system. What is important is to be in the right system; the Divine System or the Worlds System?

Why do we need a system?

*"Today, systems thinking is needed more than ever because we are becoming overwhelmed by complexity."*⁵⁴ The problem with the 'information age' is there is too much information. We need to embrace the 'wisdom age' where we have systems to manage the information.

---

⁵⁰ Ibid.
⁵¹ Covey, *The 8th Habit*: 235.
⁵² Ibid., 234.
⁵³ Ibid., 239.
⁵⁴ Senge, *The Fifth Discipline*: 69.

We need a system because:

> "...system thinking is the fifth discipline. It is the discipline that integrates the disciplines... by enhancing each of the other disciplines; it continually reminds us that the whole can exceed the sum of its parts."[55]

Dr. Edward De Bono writes on thinking skills. He is possibly best known for his 'six thinking hats' or introducing the word 'lateral thinking' into the dictionary. One of those hats is the blue hat.[56] Whilst wearing this hat, you think about the thinking. It forms a plan of how you will think through a particular matter. In the same way the system is the 'discipline that integrates the disciplines.' In this way, the 'whole can exceed the sum of its parts (See Covey's habit: Synergy.[57])

We need a system because it puts wheels on our vision:

> "...vision without systems thinking ends up painting lovely pictures of the future with no deep understanding of the forces that must be mastered to move from here to there."[58]

We need a system because it helps us see the forest for the trees:

> "...victim of complexity...drowning in details, without a clear perspective on those details....'see the forest for the trees.' But, unfortunately for most of us when we step back we just see 'lots of trees'. We pick our favourite[sic] one or two and focus our attention and efforts for change in those."[59]

---

[55] Ibid., 12.
[56] Edward de Bono, *Teach your Child how to Think* (London: Penguin Books, 1992). 93-95.
[57] Covey, *The 7 Habits of Highly Effective People*.
[58] Senge, *The Fifth Discipline*: 12.
[59] Ibid., 127.

We need a system because it helps us achieve similar results, answering the question 'if he can do it, so can I?' *"When placed in the same system, people, however different, tend to produce similar results."*[60]

The Framework

These are the principles or rules that we put in place within the system. Every component that makes up the framework will only be as good as the system that it is placed in. Every individual component in itself may be good, but how it is used (the system) determines its ultimate value. Below is a summary various frameworks. Please note that many overlap and have similarities, but different names. The comments following the titles are my understanding of the principles.

Built to Last, by Jim Collins & Jerry I. Porras

Chapter 2 – Clock building, not time telling. The key word in this principle is 'building'. This carries the sense that we should build for the long-term. A similar concept to: 'you can give a man a fish for one meal or you can teach him how to fish so he can eat the rest of his life.'

Chapter 3 – More than Profits. Behind 'more than profit' is the principle that there need to be a purpose beyond a self-serving one.

Chapter 4 - Preserve the Core/stimulate progress. This is a principle about handling change. There is only one thing that should not change and that is *"the only sacred cow in an organization should be its basic philosophy of doing business. (Thomas J. Watson, JR.)"*[61] We should not compromise our core philosophy, but rather hold true to it while everything else can change.

Chapter 5 - Big Hairy Audacious Goals The principle of goal setting. They must be big (offering a challenge), hairy (scary and taking you out of your comfort zone), and audacious by not only proclaiming it but meaning it.

Chapter 6 - Cult like Cultures. Words like loyalty, commitment and buy-in are in this principle. This principle says that if you want to last you must have stronger indoctrination, greater tightness of fit and greater elitism.

---

[60] Ibid., 42.
[61] Jim Collins, *Built to Last*: 81.

Chapter 7 - Try a lot of stuff and keep what works. This is the principle of purposeful evolution. It carries the idea that in evolution lots of the same species go about what they do and some evolve into something more useful. It's like the shot-gun approach. Just point the rifle in the general direction and some of the spray of pellets will hit the target. For the door-to-door sales person, they have to knock on 'x' amount of doors to get one sale.

Chapter 8 - Home grown Management. This principle needs little explanation. It is the principle of promoting, only from within.

Chapter 9 - Good enough is never enough. This principle puts to flight the one that says, 'close enough is good enough.' There is but one thing that will take us beyond good, maybe two: Discipline and a constant sense of discontent.

Chapter 10 - The end of the beginning. This principle says the little beginnings turn into bigger things. Those small insignificant things turn out to be the most important. The Bible teaches this one when it speaks of the importance of the corner stone (Matt.21:42, Acts 4:11, 1Pet.2:7) and in this verse: *"Take heed that you do not despise one of these little ones."* (Mat 18:10a)

Chapter 11 - Building the vision. The principle of seeing or visualizing the purpose.

Good to Great, by Jim Collins

First who... then what. *"..first got the right people on the bus, the wrong people off the bus, and the right people in the right seats – before they figured out where to drive it."* (Pg.13)

Confront the brutal facts. *"the Stockdale Paradox: You must maintain unwavering faith that you can and will prevail in the end....and at the same time have the discipline to confront the most brutal facts of your current reality, ..."* (Pg.13)

The Hedgehog Concept. *"...requires transcending the curse of competence."* (Pg13) the place where three circles overlap, what you are deeply passionate about, what drives your economic engine, and what you can be the best in the world at, is the 'sweet spot' where you are better than your competencies.

A culture of discipline. *"when you combine a culture of discipline with an ethic of entrepreneurship, you get the magical alchemy of great performance."* (Pg13)

Technology accelerators. *"...carefully selected technologies."* (Pg13) Technology isn't used just because it is there. It is used only if it helps.

The flywheel and the doom loop. *"...relentlessly pushing a giant heavy flywheel in one direction, turn upon turn, building momentum until a point of breakthrough, and beyond."* (Pg14) This is the principle of purposeful, hard work, and the use of momentum.

Life Strategies, by Dr Phillip C McGraw

Get real. *"life laws are the rules of the game. No one is going to ask you if you think these laws are fair, or if they think they should exist. Like the law of gravity, they simply are. You don't get a vote."* Pg32. To have a reality check, find out the laws of life.

You either get it, or you don't. Crack the code of human nature. Find out what makes you tick, and what makes others tick. *"so just as knowledge is power, the lack of knowledge, or a reliance upon misinformation, is crippling, misleading, and harmful."* Pg55

You create your own experience. *"You are accountable for your life. Good or bad, successful or unsuccessful, happy or sad, fair or unfair, you own your life."* Pg56

People do what works. In other words, people do what has a payoff. The payoff might be psychological, spiritual, physical, achievement or social. Payoffs can be addictive. *"Bottom line: you are shaping your own behavior by the payoffs you are getting in life. Find and control the payoffs, and you control the behavior."* Pg108

You can't change what you don't acknowledge. *"if you're unwilling to acknowledge a thought, circumstance, problem, condition, behavior, or emotions – if you won't take ownership of your role in a situation – then you cannot and will not change."* Pg109

Life rewards action. *"Make careful decisions and then pull the trigger."* Pg127 Good intentions don't count.

There is no reality, only perception. *"Accepting this law means that you embrace the fact that, no matter what happens in your life, how you interpret that event is up to you."* Pg150

Life is managed, it is not cured. *"Simply put, never in your life are you without problems and challenges."* Pg167

We teach people how to treat us. This law *"deals specifically with how you define your relationships."* Pg184

<u>There is power in forgiveness.</u> *"The power of forgiveness is the power to set yourself free from the bonds of hatred, anger, and resentment."* Pg210

<u>You have to name it to claim it.</u> *"Get clear about what you want, and take your turn."* Pg211 Set specific goals.

The 7 Habits of Highly Effective People, by Stephen R. Covey

Private victory

- Habit 1 – Be Proactive: principles of personal vision
- Habit 2 – Begin with the end in mind: principles of personal leadership
- Habit 3 – Put First Things First: principles of personal management

Public Victory

- Habit 4 – Think Win/Win: principles of interpersonal leadership
- Habit 5 – Seek First to Understand, Then to be Understood: principles of empathetic communication
- Habit 6 – Synergize: principles of creative cooperation

Renewal

- Habit 7 – Sharpen the Saw: principles of balanced self-renewal

The 8th Habit, by Stephen R. Covey

<u>Find your voice:</u> discover and express your voice.

<u>Inspire others to find their voice:</u> influence, trust, blending voices, one voice. Alignment and empowering, the age of wisdom.

The Platform

There are many systems, but operationally, all is a System. It is the way the universe was created and all Personal Development principles, or natural laws operate by it. There are many 'frameworks' that, firstly work as a system, and secondly, differ in name, but say the same things in various ways. A platform can house any number of various frameworks on it. The different frameworks don't alter the platform. There is only one sound and solid platform, and that is found in the New Testament book, 2 Peter 1:3-8.

The Holy Bible

> *"according as His divine power has given to us all things that pertain to life and godliness, through the knowledge of Him who has called us to glory and virtue, through which He has given to us exceedingly great and precious promises, so that by these you might be partakers of the divine nature, having escaped the corruption that is in the world through lust. But also in this very thing, bringing in all diligence, **filling out your faith with virtue, and with virtue, knowledge; and with knowledge self-control, and with self-control, patience, and with patience, godliness, and with godliness, brotherly kindness, and with brotherly kindness, love.** For if these things are in you and abound, they make you to be neither idle nor unfruitful in the knowledge of our Lord Jesus Christ."* (2Pe 1:3-8)

To live 'according as His divine power' you must firstly be a believer. If not a believer, you have no access to the use of divine power, nor even any understanding of the things of God and particularly His Word, try as you may. Not being plugged into the System, you cannot even be part of it, but rather you are part of this worlds system which among other more sinister things excludes you from being an empowered part of the Divine System of Personal Development.

The Bible says, *"But the natural man does not receive the things of the Spirit of God, for they are foolishness to him; neither can he know them, because they are spiritually discerned."* (1Co 2:14). Dr Barnhouse adds, *"If we are going to understand the Word of God, we must have a spiritual attitude towards it."*[62]

---

[62] Donald Grey Barnhouse, *The Invisable War* (Grand Rapids, Michigan: Zondervan Publishing House, 1965). 11.

If I haven't lost you already, I may lose you, from this point on, but, don't let that stop you from continuing, just in case you decide to become a believer.

The material presented in this book from this paragraph to the end is conceivable and fully understandable to the believer only. The book of 2 Peter was written to believers and they are spiritual in nature. Therefore, as a non-believer, your spirit has not been quickened so any spiritual discussion is about as useful as talking to a gravestone or a hip pocket in a pair of underwear. This can be changed in the next few minutes – 'with all speed'.

Faith alone, in Christ alone, is your only issue. *"He who believes on the Son has everlasting life, and he who does not believe the Son shall not see life, but the wrath of God abides upon him."* (Joh 3:36). Turn now to the back of this book to find a prayer that will make you a believer.

Even so, when the non-believer reads spiritual things, though unable to comprehend it completely, it can still have an effect on his life. I would encourage you to read on anyway.

If a believer, before you can partake you must 'rebound' *("If we confess our sins, He is faithful and just to forgive us our sins, and to cleanse us from all unrighteousness 1Jn 1:9)* in order to become empowered in the Divine System. In order to stay plugged in to the System and empowered, the believer must 'rebound' as soon as and every time he falls into carnality.

The result of 'rebound' is being in restored to full fellowship with Christ. *"The Lord says that the anointing by the Spirit renders us capable of understanding, so that we do not need to have any one teach us."*[63] From this position we can receive this promise: *"But the anointing which you received from Him abides in you, and you do not need anyone to teach you. But as*

---

[63] Ibid., 12.

His anointing teaches you concerning all things, and is true and no lie, and as He has taught you, abide in Him." (1Jn 2:27)

From here, let's go back to our text in 2 Peter, but starting from Verse 2 and following to verse 4.

> *"Grace and peace be multiplied to you through the knowledge of God and of Jesus our Lord, (3) according as His divine power has given to us all things that pertain to life and godliness, through the knowledge of Him who has called us to glory and virtue, (4) through which He has given to us exceedingly great and precious promises, so that by these you might be partakers of the divine nature, having escaped the corruption that is in the world through lust."* (2Pe 1:2-4)

> **Parallax:** *"the apparent displacement of an observed object due to a change in the position of the observer."*

Because we are referring to Scripture, what follows is a *"more reliable word of prophecy."*[64] It is more reliable than any other system of Personal Development. What we will be examining from this point on is doctrine from the canon of scripture which is more real than anything seen or heard (faith is required to have any appreciation for this) and totally reliable, meaning 'it works'. This passage in 2 Peter is saying to us that *"You have never had a failure that Bible Doctrine cannot provide a solution."*[65]

The 'how to' use this system is given to us in the first word in verse two – Grace

Grace means unmerited favour. This perhaps is the most difficult parallax to experience. Unmerited means that God gives all of these things freely, without any strings attached and

---

[64] Jr R. B. Thieme, 445-0001, (texas: R. B. Thieme, Jr., Bible Ministries, 1972).
[65] Ibid.

totally undeservingly. Grace is given based on God's character, not ours.

There is nothing, including human good that can win God's grace. The Bible doesn't teach us to 'do' things in order to gain favour with God. It teaches grace, which is all about what God does.

The following seven, normally called the chorus of seven (I will explain why it is given this title later on): faith, virtue, knowledge, self-control, patience, brotherly kindness, and love, I will rename 'The Seven Graces.' These are the seven graces that provide peace and multiply in value as our knowledge of God through the study of Bible doctrine increases.

Verse 3 says, *"according as His divine power has given to us all things that pertain to life and godliness, through the knowledge of Him who has called us to glory and virtue,"*

Grace is emphasized here again: '*according to His* divine power has given to us.' Gaining these 'graces' is all about Him, not us.

This verse is also the Bibles 'blank check' that God gives to us. The amount filled in is decided by us and can only be written in the currency of God. Our decision on the amount can only be decided by the amount of 'things pertaining to' (Bible doctrine) that we have taken in, or have knowledge of, and the currency is in God's original 'life and godliness'.

The words 'Pertaining to life' tell us that these things (the seven graces) are for right now, not the future. The only limits on this Personal Development program is placed there by us, not God. This Personal Development program promises us a fuller life than we can imagine because we are, or should be constantly increasing our knowledge of God, and the power to live a godly life whilst residing in an ungodly world.

It is 'through the knowledge (επιγυωοιζ – *recognition by implication full discernment, acknowledging)*[66] *of Him'*, the acknowledgement of God and Jesus Christ our Lord that we get this 'blank check.'

Verse 4 says, *"through which He has given to us exceedingly great and precious promises, so that by these you might be partakers of the divine nature, having escaped the corruption that is in the world through lust."*

The promises given to believers are exceedingly great. In the Greek language, exceedingly great is 'mega megesta', which means a fantastic number of and extremely valuable favours. It is by these mega megesta favours that we might become something we are not right now. That's another way of saying this Personal Development program will cause you to change.

We are not talking about the potential to change. This is actual real and lasting change. This change is only possible because the believer becomes a partaker, or partner of the Divine nature. Previous to becoming a believer, mankind is born with and controlled by the old sin nature. As a believer, the old sin nature is still there, but now so is the Divine nature which has the power in the believer's life.

Because of this acknowledgement He has *"given us exceedingly great and precious promises"*… through His Word, *"that by these"* we can be empowered in the Divine System. Not only that, *"But also in this very thing, bring in all diligence* (οπουοη – *speed, that is, dispatch, eagerness, earnestness), filling* (επινοοηυεω. – *to furnish besides, that is, fully supply, aid or contribute) out your faith"*.

There is one more word that we need to examine before we look at the seven graces or the chorus of seven. This is a key

---

[66] I will use occasionally Greek words which are found in the New Testament.

word that holds the secret to understanding the rest of these graces or chorus'. That word is 'add' or in the Modern King James Version 'filling'. In the Greek this word is epichorēgeō (*ep-ee-khor-ayg-eh'-o).* It has already been mention in the last paragraph with its definition: 'to furnish besides, that is, fully supply, aid or contribute.' It is an old Greek word that was used in reference to the payment of the expense for the Chorus (Choir) in a Greek tragedy[67]. Pay the wages for performers for one year, in advance. It is difficult to find a single word that puts this meaning into our text. The best I have heard is: 'But also in this very thing, bring in all diligence, **supplying** your faith…' Each of the chorus of seven has been fully supplied to the believer and the believer will come to know what that means as he 'inhales' Bible doctrine with the regularity of breathing. This is why the amount the believer writes on the blank check is determined by the amount of Bible Doctrine he has taken into his life.

The rest of this section will look at each of these '…very thing, bringing all diligence…', meaning a study of the seven graces[68] that make up the real platform of Personal Development that operates perfectly within the created system. As the New Testament was written in common Greek, the full meaning of these seven 'graces' cannot be captured by just using the English translation. As an introduction I will first identify what the Greek word is. Greek is a one of the most exact languages available and where one word in English has one, or even several meanings, the Greek can have many multiples of meanings, depending on the context, tone, emphasis and many

---

[67] Greek Tragedy - Aristotle defined it as: an imitation of an action(acting out on the stage some facet of life.), a serious drama, complete, and of a certain magnitude, in language embellished with each kind of artistic ornament. In simplest of terms a Greek tragedy is what now known as a play.

[68] More commonly known as the chorus of seven.

other words, something that you need to be a student of Greek to understand.

Next to each key word, I have included the actual Greek, what it looks like in English and how it is pronounced. This will be followed by the meaning from Strong's Hebrew and Greek Dictionary and last of all the Collins Pocket English Dictionary definition.

The first word to examine is the shortest word, used the most, and has the longest definition in our text – 2 Peter 1: 5f. That word is 'to.' In the original Greek, this word isn't even there, but the translators placed it there to help the text's legibility. In the Interlinear, the word 'to', becomes 'in yet the'.

To – (ἐν, en, *en)* A primary preposition denoting (fixed) *position* (in place, time or state), and (by implication) *instrumentality* (medially or constructively), that is, a relation of *rest*... Often used in compounds, with substantially the same import; rarely with verbs of motion, and then not to indicate direction, except (elliptically) by a separate (and different) prep.

Towards, used to mark the indirect object or infinitive of a verb, as far as, used to indicate equality or comparison.

Interlinear – 'in yet the'

Faith – (πίστις, pistis, *pis'-tis)* persuasion, that is, *credence*; moral *conviction* (of *religious* truth, or the truthfulness of God or a religious teacher), especially *reliance* upon Christ for salvation; abstractly *constancy* in such profession; by extension the system of religious (Gospel) *truth* itself: - assurance, belief, believe, faith, fidelity.

Strong belief, esp. without proof. Religion. Complete confidence or trust. Allegiance to a person or cause.

'in yet the'

Virtue (ἀρέτη, aretē, *ar-et'-ay)*Properly *manliness* (*valor*), that is, *excellence* (intrinsic or attributed): - praise, virtue.

Moral goodness, positive moral quality, merit

'in yet the'

Knowledge – (γνῶσις, gnōsis, *gno'-sis)* *Knowing* (the act), that is, (by implication) *knowledge:* - knowledge, science.

Facts or experience known by a person, state of knowing, specific information on a subject.

'in yet the' Inholding

Self-control – (ἐγκράτεια, egkrateia, *eng-krat'-i-ah) self control* (especially *continence*): - temperance.

Ability to control ones emotions and reactions

'in yet the' Inholding

Patience – (ὑπομονή, hupomonē, *hoop-om-on-ay')* Cheerful (or hopeful) *endurance, constancy:* - enduring, patience, patient continuance (waiting).

Patient: Enduring difficulties or delays calmly. Patience: the quality of being patient.

'in yet the' Under remaining

Godliness – (εὐσέβεια, eusebeia, *yoo-seb'-i-ah) Piety*; specifically the *gospel* scheme: - godliness, holiness.

Pious and devout to God

'in yet the' Under remaining

Brotherly kindness – (φιλαδελφία, Philadelphia, *fil-ad-el-fee'-ah) Fraternal affection:* - brotherly love (kindness), love of the brethren.

Brotherhood: Fellowship, association, Kindness: considerate, friendly, and helpful

'in yet the' Devoutedness of fond.

Love – (ἀγάπη, agapē, *ag-ah'-pay) Love,* that is, *affection* or *benevolence*; specifically (plural) a *love feast:* - (feast of) charity ([-ably]), dear, love.

Have great affection for (this definition has 8 meanings ranging from sexual passion to a score of nothing in tennis).

More on God's Personal Development System

Below is a modified diagram (the concept is originally designed by R. B. Thieme Jr. from his book 'Christian Integrity.[69]') of the Christians Personal Development System (CPDS). This chapter provides a description of the CPDS without going into too much detail. Each component of this System and the tools requiring development are the subject of another book. Here, the reader can get an idea of what the CPDS looks like and at the very least, get started.

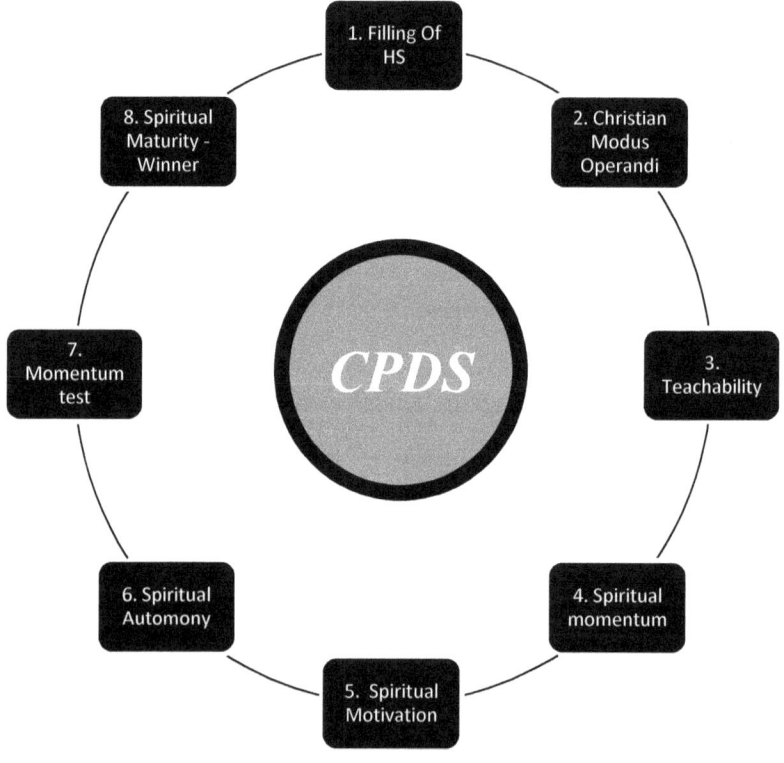

---

[69] Jr R. B. Thieme, *Christian Integrity* (Houston Texas: R. B. Thieme Jr. Bible Ministries, 2002, 1997, 1984).

Each component of this system has a descriptor, which without further teaching means very little, if anything to the reader. What I can do here though is explain how each component functions. Think of each component as a Locke, not too different from the ones in the Panama Canal. This is a way for large ships to travel up hill, not too different from our personal development journey.

The ship enters the first Locke and a gate closes behind it. Then water is pumped into the Locke which raises the ship to the next level, The front gate opens and the ship sails along the canal to the next Locke where the process continues. It almost goes without saying that once the ship has to go down levels, they don't just put it on a water slide and let her rip! The same process is followed.

Think of the CPDS functioning in the same way noting that there is only one entry point – Locke 1: The filling of the Holy Spirit. As mentioned before, this term may not mean much to some readers, so in its most basic form, to even start on the CPDS, you must be born again. You must be a believer, at which point you are filled with the Holy Spirit. This is the gate of entry into the whole system.

For the believer, to stay in the system, you must utilise the devises that God provides. Thieme calls these the Ten Problem Solving Devices. (See the next diagram.)

The degree in which you know and use these devises, determines the level of success gained within the system, the speed in which you travel through the system, and the quality of results you receive from the system.

These devices form an inner shield that protects you from outside pressures and obstacles that life has a way of putting in our way. With this protection, you are able to continue in the CPDS for the rest of your life on earth.

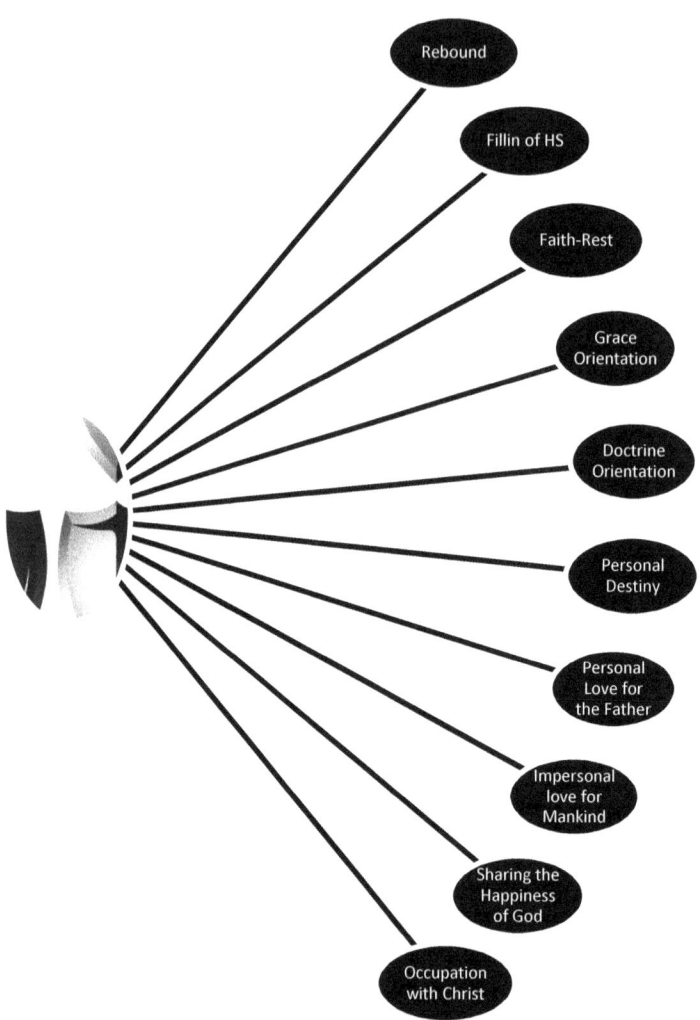

Again, the terms identifying each device may or may not mean much at this point, but the diagram illustrates the function. The ideal situation is where all ten devices are operational, but realistically this is not the case for anyone. If you are exempt from this last statement, please 'beam yourself up Scotty' through the book and into my lounge room.

In the following diagram, I have combined the two previous ones.

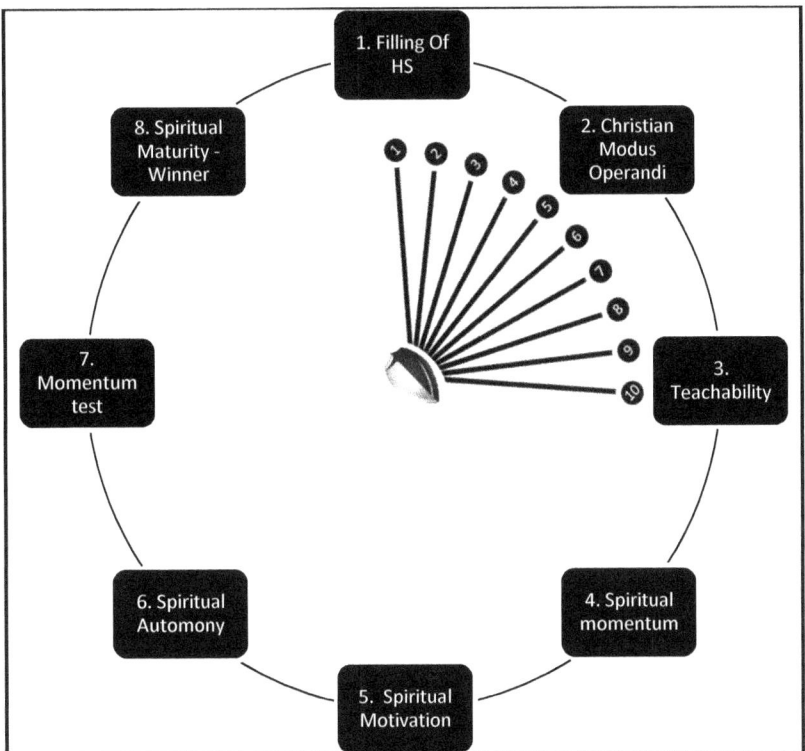

The way the ten devices work is by spinning on the shield in the centre so that they are applied at any point in the system. Allow me to give you an example.

Let me introduce you to a fictitious person we will call G.I. Joe. He is a believer that not unlike any other believer makes mistakes. We will call this mistake 'sin.' G. I. Joe knows that every time he 'sins', he is out of fellowship with God, or put another way, out of the CPDS. He is aware that if he applies 1John 1:9 (*"If we confess our sins, He is faithful and just to forgive us our sins, and to cleanse us from all unrighteousness."*), the 'rebound device', he will instantaneously be brought back into fellowship with God, filled with the Spirit, and back into the CPDS.

G. I. Joe discovers a problem though. He keeps doing the same sin over and over again and he keeps using the rebound device and gets frustrated because he isn't making any progress. He is just 'spinning his wheels'. The 'rebound' device helps but is proving to be not enough.

Over time, he begins to develop some other devices. Devises like 'faith-rest' and a sense of 'personal destiny', as well as 'doctrine orientation' and a 'personal love for God'.

Now, that sin that kept repeating itself is a distant memory. By the use of multiple problem solving devices, G. I. Joe has overcome this problem and is moving on in his CPDS.

When G. I. Joe Comes to the next Locke: Christian Modus Operandi, he has the power to live the Christian way of life, in the face of pressure to do otherwise, because he has numerous devises (bullets in the gun) to fight with.

And so, his journey continues, picking up more devices as he goes through each Locke of the CPDS.

This brings us back to the end of the previous chapter. Every believer needs to develop a platform in their lives that enables them to best develop the devices to operate in the system. That platform is described for us in 2 Peter 1:2-8. Come with me as we look, in detail, at this platform.

Faith

Paraphrase/Translation

*"4 And by the same mighty power He has given us all the other rich and wonderful blessings He promised; for instance, the promise to save us from the lust and rottenness all around us, and to give us His own character. 5 But to obtain these gifts, you need more than **faith**; you must also work hard to be good..."*[70]

*"4 By means of these He has bestowed on us His precious and exceedingly great promises, so that through them you may escape [by flight] from the moral decay (rottenness and corruption) that is in the world because of covetousness (lust and greed), and become sharers (partakers) of the divine nature. 5 For this very reason, adding your diligence [to the divine promise], employ every effort in exercising your **faith** to develop virtue..."*[71]

Faith – (πίστις, pistis, *pis'-tis*) persuasion, that is, *credence*; moral *conviction* (of *religious* truth, or the truthfulness of God or a religious teacher), especially *reliance* upon Christ for salvation; abstractly *constancy* in such profession; by extension the system of religious (Gospel) *truth* itself: - assurance, belief, believe, faith, fidelity.

> Strong belief, especially without proof. Religion. Complete confidence or trust. Allegiance to a person or cause.

THE FIRST AND FOREMOST, indeed the action that opens the door to the rest of the Bibles Personal Development Program is faith. This is faith that has complete 'reliance upon Christ for salvation.' It is being 'saved,' 'born again,' or becoming a Christian.

---

[70] Tyndale House Publishers, *Living Letters* (Wheaton, Illinois: Tyndale House Publishers, 1962), Paraphrase.II Peter 1:4-5a

[71] Zondervan Publishing House, *The Amplified bible* (Grand Rapids, Michigan: Zondervan Publishing House, 1987).II Peter 1:4-5a

By obtaining salvation, the believer now has a relationship with God and becomes an active part of His plan, involving the rest of His Personal Development program.

There is no other way to be made active in God's plan. *"Faith alone in Christ alone"*[72] *"And there is salvation in no other One; for there is no other name under Heaven given among men by which we must be saved."* (Act 4:12)

Salvation is by grace through faith. *"For by grace you are saved through faith, and that not of yourselves, it is the gift of God, not of works, lest anyone should boast."* (Eph 2:8-9)

Faith is the only starting point, but it is only just the start. *"But, beloved, we are persuaded better things of you and things that accompany salvation, though we speak in this way."* (Heb 6:9)

There is only one way to obtain this faith and that is by hearing the Word of God. *"Then faith is of hearing, and hearing by the Word of God."* (Rom 10:17) If there is no faith or salvation, there has been no hearing of the Word of God. The Word of God is written for the spirit, which, in the non-believer is dead or yet to be quickened or awakened. Until the spirit is awakened, it is not possible (except by God revealing) to understand anything spiritual. The Word of God is spiritual. To the unbeliever, it is just a book with of historical stories. To the believer it is the book that pertains to all aspects of life.

It is a mysterious thing that God does by His Spirit for the non-believer. Though the non-believer, through anything of his own effort, cannot receive anything of the Word of God's intended value, God can use His Word and drop it into a window of the non-believers soul, enough to quicken his spirit by his positive volition towards that Word and cause him to believe on the

---

[72] Jr R. B. Thieme, "Better things for Christmas," (Houston, Texas: R. B. Thieme, Jr., Bible Ministries, 2003).

Lord Jesus Christ. Salvation has been given. Faith is his. But it is just the beginning.

Faith, the foundation is secured. Access to the Bibles Personal Development Program is given. *"Nevertheless the foundation of God stands sure, having this seal: The Lord knew those who are His. And, let everyone who names the name of Christ depart from iniquity!"* (2Ti 2:19)

> *"If we say that we have fellowship with Him and walk in darkness, we lie and do not practice the truth. But if we walk in the light, as He is in the light, we have fellowship with one another, and the blood of Jesus Christ His Son cleanses us from all sin."* (1Jn 1:6-7)

The above describes faith in respect to salvation. There is a continuing faith too. This faith is necessary for continual growth. It is faith that grows from the regular, disciplined and ever-continual taking in, or inhaling of the Word of God and Bible doctrine.

{ *Parallax: "the apparent displacement of an observed object due to a change in the position of the observer."* }

The faith of salvation provides and the continuing faith supplies. The certainty of this supply causes us to rest in that faith. Thieme calls this the 'Faith-rest' technique.

In summary, the faith-rest technique is having the inner peace that enables the believer to rest in complete trust in the God through the Bible doctrine and promises provided in His Word, no matter what the surrounding circumstances are dictating.

Getting busy, rushing about, trying to 'make it happen', and creating a sense of urgency is poles apart from having this kind of faith. The person who does not have this faith looks like the person that has had one too many energy drinks, or too much coffee. They get the shakes because there is too much energy to dispel. Their heart rate is dangerously high, and their minds work at an astonishing confused speed as they try to break through some barrier or ceiling on their performance.

> *"It takes a great deal of speed to crack the sound barrier, but to crack the faith barrier requires, not excessive speed, but simply standing still."*[73]

When the believer takes in faith, he is calm, confident and sure that what God has planned will happen and God doesn't need any help from him. He can rest:

> *"And we know that all things work together for good to those who love God, to those who are called according to His purpose."* (Rom 8:28)

> *"And the peace of God which passes all understanding shall keep your hearts and minds through Christ Jesus."* (Php 4:7)

So, let us move on to the next stage of this program.

---

[73] Jr R. B. Thieme, *The Faith-Rest Life* (Texas: R. B. Thieme Jr. Bible Ministries, 2004, 1999, 1961). 1.

Virtues

Paraphrase/Translation

5 But to obtain these gifts, you need more than faith; you must also work hard to be good..."[74]

5 For this very reason, adding your diligence [to the divine promise], employ every effort in exercising your faith to develop virtue..."[75]

Virtue (ἀρέτη, aretē, *ar-et'-ay*) Properly *manliness* (*valor*), that is, *excellence* (intrinsic or attributed): - praise, virtue.

Moral goodness, positive moral quality, merit

THIS SECTION IS BOTH IMPORTANT and is therefore proportionately larger than the previous and the following chapters. I have selected seven specific virtues to examine, together with the parallax of each. They are truth, grace, love, servant-hood, humility, justice, and self-control.

Before we look at this collection of virtues, I need to make clear that the use of the word 'virtue' in the Greek New Testament means something completely different to how we would define it today. The 'virtue' in the Bible has absolutely nothing to do with morality as the dictionary would point out. The virtue of the Bible means, *"a gracious act, a quality of goodness that belongs to God, exhale of doctrine, doctrine in the soul."*[76]

Other translations of the Bible[77] use alternative words to virtue, which helps us gain an understanding of what the word means. The James Moffatt New Testament uses 'resolution'. The Edgar

---

[74] Publishers, *Living Letters*.II Peter 1:5
[75] House, *The Amplified bible*.II Peter 1:5
[76] Jr R. B. Thieme, "445-0005," (1972).
[77] Curtis Vaughan, *The New Testament from 26 Translations* (Grand Rapids, Michigan: Zondervan Publishing House, 1967, 1977).

J. Goodspeed New Testament uses 'goodness'. The Charles B. Williams New Testament uses 'moral character'. The New American Standard Bible uses 'moral excellence', and the Richard Francis Weymouth New Testament in Modern Speech uses 'noble character'.

Virtue has to do with mighty power and valour. *"...this is the old English word which translates the Greek of a passage that speaks of 'the mighty angels'"*[78] in 2 Thessalonians 1:7 - *"and to give rest with us to you who are troubled, at the revealing of the Lord Jesus from Heaven with the angels of His power,"* (2Th 1:7)

To have virtue is to act in an unmerited fashion (grace), to act like God would (and did) and this can only come out of the believer who has 'inhaled' the Word of God to the point where they live it in their actions (exhale doctrine).

> From Built to Last (Pg72)
>
> **Words/Deeds, Numbers/Values**
>
> *"People who make the numbers and share the values go onward and upward. People who miss the numbers and share the values get a second chance. People with no values and no numbers – easy call. The problem is with those who make the numbers but don't share the values."*

It has become my belief that virtue has been confused with value. The difference is in most cases subtle, but the results are drastically different. The differences in the results are the difference between character and consequence. Virtue results in character. Values result in consequences. Personal Development is about character development, not simply applying some law of nature in order to reap the consequences.

---

[78] Barnhouse, *The Invisable War*: 128.

Truth-P-Tolerance

The parallax of truth is tolerance. The parallax of tolerance is truth. The difference between the virtue of truth and the value of tolerance is fundamental to what is at the base of why we act and make decisions.

Character	P-Virtue	P-Value	Consequences
• Opposed to falsehood and wrong-doing – The end does not justify the means • Belief in and committed to absolutes – There is right and wrong • Open to correction and conviction – I am not always right. There is only one God and it's not me. • Confidence in what is true – truth is the source of my confidence	TRUTH	TOLERANCE	• Tolerance of falsehood and wrong-doing – The end justifies the means • Pragmatic – Act according to practices/consequence rather than principle/theory • Closed to correction. Has to be right to save ego • Vacillating – The right to change your mind

Doing right by opposing wrong

Edmund Burke said, *"The only thing necessary for the triumph is for good men to do nothing."*

This quote stands as one of the unassailable truths about the need for freedom of action, in the world. It is one of the great quotes that has been used and altered to suit the multitude of definition, depending on the user. The most common alteration is; 'The only thing necessary for the triumph [of evil] is for good men to do nothing.'

The one who actively opposes 'wrong' is doing so by virtue of what is 'right' based on truth. The one who does nothing is doing so by value based on tolerance. He may as well be the one doing [evil]. In fact, he is potentially more dangerous than the evil doer.

The message of being 'tolerant' is a popular one and for the majority who think in dichotomies[79], it has its merits. Pierre Bayle wrote, *"It is thus tolerance that is the source of peace, and intolerance that is the source of disorder and squabbling."* The point here, as will be made throughout this book, is that there is only one source of real, permanent and persevering peace, and tolerance, or in a broader sense, values are not it. The result of tolerance is, 'give him and inch, and he'll take a mile.' It's a promise that 'you can take to the bank'. To secure lasting peace will involve first disorder, squabbling and often an escalation into fights. The same can be said for freedom; *"Ultimately, national freedom is maintained by military victory (2Chron. 20:27-30; Neh. 4:14)"*[80] Military action often takes place when a situation cannot be tolerated any longer.

If you are hard-wired or scripted with 'tolerance', you will interact with others accordingly. There are concerns that, if an inch is given, how far will the other go? Perhaps this is because the majorities are operating from tolerance. Consider what happens when you treat someone assumed to be operating from tolerance, when in fact they operate from truth? The person scripted to 'truth' may be left wondering why there is so much aggression? Truth trusts. Tolerance distrusts.

I have often heard, in protest to being linked to any particular religion, that most wars are started over religion. This may be true and there aren't any arguments here. Truth is by nature intolerant of that which is false, and that intolerance will cause friction, wars, and opposition. We look at the horrors of war and deem that they are a bad option. They are horrible. They are a bad option, but consider what our world would be like if we did not fight those wars or gain the freedoms we now enjoy. If we just decided to tolerate the dictatorship of a power hungry ruler, or just let an insane person murder millions of people just

---

[79] Dichotomies: division into two opposing groups or parts.
[80] R. B. Thieme, *Christian Integrity*: 70.

because of their race. If the stance of tolerance had been taken, Adolf Hitler would have dominated Europe and Britain and Japan would own Australia. Bishop Thomas Wilson expressed it well: *"truth provokes those whom it does not convert."*

Truth doesn't change, nor does it go away. *"You can bend it and twist it... You can misuse and abuse it... But even God cannot change the Truth."* (Michael Levy). I would not go as far as suggesting that there is something God cannot do. This is bordering on asking stupid questions like 'Can God make rocks so big that He cannot lift them?' Perhaps it would be better to say, 'but Truth[81] cannot be changed.' Tolerance, on the other hand is all about bending, twisting and accommodating, and results in misuse and abuse.

"The truth is incontrovertible, malice may attack it, ignorance may deride it, but in the end; there it is." (Winston Churchill)

The Truth cannot be ignored. We see this vividly in a court of law when 'ignorance is not a plea' *"Not being known doesn't stop the truth from being true."* (Richard Bach)

I do believe that, even those who are 'tolerant' scripted are really seeking and want the truth, but find themselves pursuing and expecting tolerance. In the words of Josh Billing; *"As scarce as truth is, the supply has always been in excess of the demand."* Truth is available in abundance, for those who earnestly and actively seek it. To not even seek it, results in the 'evil triumphing'.

Have you ever noticed that anything left alone gravitates to deterioration? Doing nothing always means things get worse. If a person does nothing about his health, he gets sick. If a person does not discipline his thinking, he becomes a negative thinker, or does not even have the skill of thinking.

---

[81] I use a capital 'T' because God is Truth.

By default, most live by the value of being tolerant, and deteriorate. This is a perfectly natural way to live. To live by default is just another way of saying we are living according to how mankind has lived since the fall of Adam and Eve. By choice, however, we can live according to truth, and develop.

> **Law of reciprocity**
>
> One of the earliest records of this law is found in Gen. 9:6 – *"Whoever sheds man's blood, his blood shall be shed by man; for He made man in the image of God."* A quick look at the history of the church in Japan points out many lessons, one of which is this law. 'whosoever forces a religion, will have a religion forced on them.' Here is a common quote that makes the point (excuse the pun): 'Live by the sword, die by the sword.' With a little more thought we come up with this realisation: 'Everything you do to others, you actually do to yourself.' This law is unbreakable. It cannot be changed. It is this way and our text tells us why, *'for He made man in the image of God.'* This 'law of reciprocity' is actually a part of God's character. It is fundamental to who He is. No-one will escape the enforcement of this law.
>
> *"For the day of Jehovah is near on all the nations; as you have done, it shall be done to you. Your reward shall return upon your head."* (Oba 1:15)

"Toleration is the greatest gift of the mind; it requires the same effort of the brain that it takes to balance oneself on a bicycle." (Helen Keller).

At a glance, this quote looks as though it is in support of tolerance. I guess it could be if riding a bicycle was as challenging as it would be for anyone with just a few of the disabilities possessed by Helen Keller. Personally, I haven't ridden a bicycle in years and yet I am confident that it would take about zero brain effort to get on and ride a bike. I could do it by default. We have all heard and maybe used the saying, 'it's like riding a bike', meaning that once you have learned to ride a bike, we tend to never forget it. In this light, tolerance is a mindless activity or one that requires no thought because it is the default operating system.

Have you ever been asked or told to, 'do whatever it takes,' when a goal is in front of you that needs to be achieved? For the 'tolerant ones', they will, without hesitation, say yes, because the end (the goal) justifies the means. The means, right or wrong, ethical or not, moral or immoral, will be tolerated in order to get the end.

This was a constant challenge in one sales position I held as I saw time and time again those who had 'values' give into the carrot placed before them by lying and cheating in order to achieve the goal. For the ones who possess virtue, the virtue of truth, would not answer this question without defining just what 'whatever it takes' means. The virtuous one would rather do what is right and fail in achieving the goal than achieve the goal by questionable means. The end does not justify the means. In fact, 'the end is the same as the means.' Here is an overarching principle: 'you reap what you sow,' or the law of reciprocity.

Tolerance will allow seemingly small compromises. We would do well to heed the words of Albert Einstein, *"Whoever is careless with the truth in small matters cannot be trusted with important matters."* The one who holds to 'Truth' takes care with the small matters. It is not the devil in the detail. The God of Truth is.

Belief

Think about 'belief' and 'absolutes'.

Any belief, with the absence of absolutes is a belief that lacks security and subject to change, given the circumstances. Strong belief can only become strong if there are absolutes. Absolutes are the very foundations for belief. Truth, the virtue, has absolutes. Tolerance, the value, has pragmatism. Pragmatism is the foundation for practices and consequences. Covey writes *"While we are free to choose our actions, we are not free to choose the consequences of those actions."*[82] Practices or actions and consequences, do not require belief. There is no need to believe in something that is a fact. Only that which requires faith needs belief.

To further simplify the above paragraph, we could say that the 'tolerant' eliminate the need for belief, yet they would not deny the importance of it. Even easier, those who deny God, the absolutely absolute, don't know what they are talking about.

Here is the truth: *"If you want good results, you need to perform good actions. If you want to perform good actions, you must have positive expectations. To have good expectations, you have to first believe. It all goes back to that... it all starts with belief."*[83]

The parallax between 'belief as a virtue' and 'belief as a value' can be difficult to see. Consider it this way. There is one person I am thinking of now, but there are many whom the reader may know as well, that knows how to quote all the Personal Development speakers and writers, yet fails to actually live by those quotes. *"Proverbs are always platitudes until you have personally experienced the truth of them."* Aldous Huxley. We know that 'we reap what we sow', but until we experience this law of reciprocity, do we really know it to be true? The proverb is truth, the platitude[84] is tolerant.

<u>Belief is important</u>. A person's belief or lack thereof *"can act as a ceiling on talent."*[85] Not only is belief important for us to realize our potential and maximize our strengths, belief has the power to make our wildest dreams come true. *"So many of our dreams at first seem impossible, then they seem improbable,*

---

[82] Covey, *The 7 Habits of Highly Effective People*.
[83] Maxwell, *Talent is never enough*.
[84] Platitude: a flat, dull, or trite remark, especially one uttered as if it were fresh or profound.
[85] Maxwell, *Talent is never enough*.

and then, when we summon the will, they soon become inevitable." (Christopher Reeve, AKA Superman). Belief is one of the driving forces to make us grow, as long as what is believed in is Truth.

What is believed in is more important.

People say they believe in many things including the company they work for, cars, football teams, grocery stores and sometimes politicians. To say we believe in any of these things is a gross misuse and weak use of the word. Actually, we tolerate all these, because as soon as a better one (in our own opinion) comes along, we change camps. I was a Ford fan, until I drove a Holden. I tolerated (even though it looked like believed in) that, until I drove a Mazda. What do you call a constantly changing belief? I'm not too sure, but it's not belief. Belief as in Truth is changeless. So if I can so readily change my preferences, I must be tolerating them. Now I will easily tolerate driving a Jaguar or riding a Harley Davidson.

One belief that is promoted in the great halls of Personal Development universities in a big way is the belief in self. I will quote John Maxwell again here with, *"When it comes to believing in themselves, some people are agnostic. That's not only a shame, it also keeps them from becoming what they could be."* [86]

There is only One sure thing to believe in, and that is Truth. This does not mean to say that those who are agnostic cannot achieve, or that belief in self is not all that it is cranked up to be. We are yet to see the limits of the power of belief in self, but there are limits. At some point, the body will not take any more fitness or weight loss although we will usually quit before it comes to that (self-imposed limit). At some point the mind will go from genius to insane. We may not have identified those limits and we may even be a great distance from even reaching

---

[86] Ibid.

those limits, but there are limits, unless our belief is in the One that has no limits. We have a word for something beyond limits – miracles.

Only One Truth – stand corrected.

I once heard it said, 'you know your own truth.' We were being asked a rhetorical question which required an honest answer (just another way of trying to tell yourself the truth). *"What you perceive, your observations, feelings, interpretations, are all your truth. Your truth is important. Yet it is not The Truth."* (Linda Ellinor). For some, that is a hard saying. Our perceptions, observations, feelings and interpretations of life form a strong source for what is believed to be true and we eagerly invest our ego in being right. Being right also means that we are not wrong, and we quickly become closed to correction. If we invest sufficient amounts of ego, we dare not admit error. The loss would be too great, so we take the next best option and tolerate rather than switch to truth. What quickly happens is what Covey calls win/lose, lose/win or lose/lose.

> *Parallax: "the apparent displacement of an observed object due to a change in the position of the observer."*

At my 21st surprise birthday party, my friends thought it would be fun to throw me in the pool. My friends were big bikers and it was clear that I was going to lose this fight and end up wet. My wife was so confident in my demise; she even brought a change of clothes in anticipation of seeing me unceremoniously soaked. I did end up wet, but so did four of those bikers. If I was going to lose, I was taking as many with me as I could – lose/lose, but fun. Whether it was right or wrong to plan such a scheme was quickly forgotten. It became all about ego. If I couldn't save my own, I was determined to crash a few others. In hindsight, the virtuous way to handle this would have been to just jump into the pool myself, like any good kamikaze.

To be closed to correction means a tolerance towards the source of correction is demonstrated. To be open to correction means the truth, the source of correction is able help in further development. J. L. Borges said, *"Truth never penetrates the unwilling mind."*

The Bible says, *"Jesus said to him, I am the Way, the Truth, and the Life; no one comes to the Father but by Me."* (Joh 14:6) Notice that central to the Way and the Life is the Truth. It doesn't say 'I am the Truth, the way and the life', nor does it say I, 'I am life, the way and the truth.' The Truth is central.

Confidence

They say it's a woman's prerogative to change her mind. Actually, anyone has the ability to change their mind. Perhaps my reader is thinking of someone who constantly does so. How much confidence do you have in this person? How much confidence do they have in themselves? If you want to fight for this right, go right ahead and destroy your own self-confidence because that is what vacillating[87] will do. Rather than call this a negative activity, we tolerate it. Personally, I don't like feeling tolerated, so I would rather stand on the side of truth as a source of confidence. To be known as a person of his/her word is a great virtue. To be a person who keeps commitments and is trusted is a great honour.

> *"Unless your heart, your soul, and your whole being are behind every decision you make, the words from your mouth will be empty, and each action will be meaningless. Truth and confidence are the roots of happiness."* (Mark Twain)

The fundamental Personal Development principle here is:

> *"We are true to who we say we are and what we claim to be. We refuse to lie, deceive, cheat, or in any way*

---

[87] Vacillating: not resolute, wavering, indecisive, hesitating.

> *erode what is true by either action or attitude. The character we develop as people of the truth is marked by integrity, reliability, and transparency."*[88]

Whilst reading this, and having examined your core beliefs, you may have found that you relate more to tolerance than truth. You might then agree that a change is required.

The Bible says, *"And you shall know the truth, and the truth shall make you free."* (Joh 8:32) The Truth is God. The God that must be acknowledged as Lord of your life. Jesus said, *"... I am the Way, the Truth, and the Life; no one comes to the Father but by Me."* (Joh 14:6)

A lesson from the history of the Roman Empire can be seen here:

> *"In general, Roman policies toward the religion and customs of conquered people were rather tolerant... but the Roman brand of tolerance could not reconcile what appeared to be the obstinacy of the Jews, who insisted on worshiping only their God."*[89]

Tolerance cannot stand up to the truth.

---

[88] Joseph M. Stowell, *Eternity: Reclaiming a passion for what endures* (Grand Rapids: Discovery House Publishers, 2006).
[89] Gonzalez, *The Story of Christianity*, 1: 15.

Grace-P-Greed

Grace means 'favour or good will, mercy, clemency, pardon'. It can also mean gift. The parallax of grace is greed. Greed means 'excessive or rapacious[90] desire'. The parallax of greed is grace.

Character	P-Virtue	P-Value	Consequences
• Uses power to empower others to succeed • Generous • Merciful • Forgiving.	GRACE	GREED	• Uses power for personal gain at other' expense • Economic/Pride • Justice/Ruthless • Vengeful.

The previous chapter, Truth P Tolerance, found truth to be both final and firm. Grace, on the other hand, is a virtue that enables and encourages us to come to our full potential, in truth. It is often seen as 'soft' and so opposite thinking is adopted. What is needed is a parallax thinking to take place.

The character traits of the graceful are seen in the way they use power, their generosity, mercifulness and forgiveness. Should a person find they are using power for their own gain, or at the expense of others, they are not operating out of virtue of grace. They are not seen as having character, but consequence that comes from the value of greed. Consequences are the result of a decision made or action taken. We may be free to choose or act, but the consequences are by default of those choices and actions.

Perhaps a painful situation has taken place. Your decision and following action will be on the side of virtue, or on the side of

---

[90] Rapacious: Given to seizing for plunder or the satisfaction of greed, inordinately greedy, predatory; extortionate, (for animals) subsisting by the capture of living prey; predacious.

value. If on the side of virtue, character is developed. If on the side of value, consequences are forthcoming. It was Covey who penned, *"The price must be paid and the process followed. You always reap what you sow; there is no shortcut."*[91]

If generosity is a challenging way to behave, you may assume that greed is the way you are hard-wired. Can't forgive someone? You are struggling with the difference between a virtue and a value, between character and consequence.

At a glance the difference between grace and greed is massive. Grace is patient/greed is impatient, Grace listens/greed ignores, Grace understands/greed misunderstands, Grace sees potential/greed sees weakness. It is the line that separates the two that is thin and barely noticeable. We can see this thin line by the way power and resources are used. The way generosity, mercy and forgiveness are implemented. This thin line is but a decision to act.

The use of power

<u>What is power?</u>

To most, power is what runs through some wires and turns the lights on. To others, power is the force that propels their vehicle into motion. To Henry Kissinger, *"power is the ultimate aphrodisiac"* (Kissinger, And I Quote). It was Francis Bacon who said, *"Knowledge is power"* (Bacon, Meditations Sacrae).

Power can be confused with something else. Take authority as an example. *"Authority and power are two different things: power is the force by means of which you can oblige others to obey you. Authority is the right to direct and command, to be listened to or obeyed by others. Authority requests power. Power without authority is tyranny."* (Jacques Maritain, "The Democratic Charter," Man and the State).

---

[91] Covey, *The 7 Habits of Highly Effective People.*

The best definition of power I have come across is; 'power is the force by means of which...' The first dictionary definition is 'ability to do or act; capability of doing or accomplishing something.' Power is a force. It is a force that we can possess, as well as a force that we can pretend to have. *"Power is not only what you have but what the enemy thinks you have."* (Saul Alinsky, Tactics, Rules for Radicals). Often we can deem a person to have power just by *"One of the things about powerful people is they have the ability to make it look easy."* (Ice-T, Men's Health, Dec. 2005)

> *Parallax: "the apparent displacement of an observed object due to a change in the position of the observer."*

How is it obtained

As Ice-T put it, power can be obtained by 'making it look easy' or making whatever the task, that may be seen as difficult or complex, look like you can do it blindfolded. This kind of power is power placed in someone by another. That someone may or may not have any power claimed to be their own.

Power can be borrowed. People do this all the time, especially on their Resumes. If they worked for a highly esteemed company, they will sell that point for whatever they can to make themselves look better for the position being sought, or how about the name of the Managing Director that is there as a reference?

I have a signed copy of Tom Hopkins famous book on sales. Does that make me a great sales person? I think not. Sales are not part of my collection of skills and strengths and as such, I am tempted to borrow the strength of another, in order to compensate. What I won't tell you is that I purchased that book at a book fair for $2. Oops! I just told you, didn't I? Try to remember, *"But borrowing strength builds weakness."*[92]

Power can be bestowed. Perhaps a position that carries authority and decision making power has been given, or your role is one of leadership. Power is necessary for you to carry out the task. This is the sort of power given to the Prime Minister, or the President. Imagine how well it would go if they forgot that the only reason they have such power is because the majority voted for them. See how power quickly disappears along with the position.

However it is obtained, we can conclude that power is not something we are born with and those that have it would do well to remember it. Those who have forgotten this now form a trail of poor leadership litter going back as far as you like in history.

I am reminded of a simple but favourite story. It's about the turtle that was found sitting high on a fencepost. The only way he could have got there was with the help of others.

> *"Perhaps those who are best suited to power are those who have never sought it. Those who ... have leadership thrust upon them, and take up the mantle because they must, and find to their own surprise that they wear it well."* (J. K. Rowling, Harry Potter and the Deathly Hallows).

The purpose of power

I wrote earlier that we are not born with power. As we begin to grow though, so does a power: the power of choice. Here we attach the purpose to power. This is choice to use power for the empowerment of others or power for personal gain. How you and I will use power is determined by our core drivers: grace the virtue or greed the value.

---

[92] Ibid.

"Power has only one duty -- to secure the social welfare of the People." (Benjamin Disraeli, Sybil).

Generosity

> *"It has always seemed strange to me... the things we admire in men, kindness and generosity, openness, honesty, understanding and feeling, are the concomitants[93] of failure in our system. And those traits we detest, sharpness, greed, acquisitiveness, meanness, egotism and self-interest, are the traits of success. And while men admire the quality of the first they love the produce of the second."* (John Steinbeck).

Men will admire 'the first' and produce the 'second' because they are at the basic level greedy by default (old sin nature) rather than gracious. Men know that all things gracious are to be sought after, but left to their own fantastic devises, still end up greedy.

Generosity can be like a mask. Horace Mann wrote,

> *"Generosity during life is a very different thing from generosity in the hour of death; one proceeds from genuine liberality and benevolence, the other from pride or fear."*

Here is an interesting introduction of words to our discussion. Words like benevolence, pride, and fear. These are words that describe deep seated motives. Motives: that are stronger at various times of life. Motives: that shows themselves as, generosity. Generous in the time of life from genuine liberality and benevolence, and then when the hour of death is upon us, generous out of pride and/or fear.

How many promises of wealth or great inheritance, have been made for 'when I die'? This is a common example of

---

[93] Concomitants: existing or occurring with something else, often in a lesser way; accompanying.

'conditional generosity' or 'putting on the appearance of generosity'. Usually, there is a condition of being good, or upholding a tradition etc... If this is the total effect of efforts in the development of self, over a lifetime, I do believe something was missed.

It is well said, *"He who gives what he would as readily throw away, gives without generosity; for the essence of generosity is in self sacrifice."* (Henry Taylor). Self sacrifice verses self preservation will determine generosity or economy.

Mercy

Mercy is not justice. Justice has no mercy. The time of this writing is the 3rd of May 2011, the day after the news that the world's most wanted man, Osama Bin Laden has been killed. The president of the United States of America announced, among other things, that justice has been done. Justice is what is being sought and there is zero tolerance to the word mercy. There is no clearer example that shows mercy and justice are so far apart. Imagine what would happen to someone who, in the midst of the party outside the White House or at Ground Zero, New York, stood up and gave a speech on how mercy should have been shown. Voltaire said it well, *"He who is merely just is severe."*

Justice (the trait of character) and mercy (the virtue) may be poles apart, but justice, on its own, without a foundation of mercy will never be sufficient. In our example, how can the extinguished life of one man, who is responsible for the death of thousands, be justice? It is probably some measure of justice, but my personal feeling is full justice cannot be achieved. Bin Laden's death doesn't bring a single person back.

The virtues outlined in this book come from who God is. The Bible describes God as being a merciful God and numerous times says His mercies endure forever. The Bible also says God is just. He is also a God of vengeance as well as of forgiveness.

We cannot come to terms with this while we are thinking right and wrong, black and white, or in opposites. We have to think in parallax. Your position in life, in as much as how you see the existence of God will determine which side of God you experience. Deny Him means getting used to the pursuit of justice. Believe in Him and you will see how merciful He is.

Has it been heard that if there was a loving God, he would not allow such injustices to happen? Perhaps these are your own words. Here is what Tozer says, *"The vague and tenuous hope that God is too kind to punish the ungodly has become a deadly opiate for the consciences of millions."* (A. W. Tozer). Let's make it clear. Gods wants each of us to be part of His family. If showing mercy won't convince or convert you, justice or judgement is the next approach. *"I tell you, brethren, if mercies and if judgments do not convert you, God has no other arrows in His quiver."* (Robert Murray M'Cheyne). I don't know about you, but I would not like to be in the place where God has tried both and I still don't respond. To be left alone by him certainly spells the end of me. I will boldly say that should God abandon anyone, they will die that instant.

Let's get back to the difference for the Personal Development practitioner. With God as the ingredient the virtue of mercy is acquired. Without God, the best one can hope to achieve is a measure of justice or put another way, you might get what you believe you deserve. There is no doubt; you will get what you deserve. What goes 'round, comes 'round. You do reap what you sow. There may be a difference between what you believe you deserve and what you actually deserve. In a word, the pursuit of what you believe you deserve, or standing up and fighting for your rights is a character trait called GREED. At the end of the day, you think it is all about you.

"I have always found that mercy bears richer fruits than strict justice." (Abraham Lincoln)

Forgiving

There was a friend who worked in the same company as I. Both of us were of the same faith. Both of us had our positions terminated for reasons of health. I recall a conversation I had with him and we started to discuss a few things that happened around our leaving the company. This is never a pleasant situation, even when the parting is on good terms. There is an opportunity to develop an unforgiving attitude towards others. Whether there is just cause for this or not is less important than what is drawn out of our own Personal Development. In this case, do I forgive or do I seek vengeance. My friend voiced his difficulty in forgiving. I was more concerned for the condition and further development of my friend than the wrongs that may or may not have been done. I was firstly reminded of what forgiveness I had experienced, making it easier to forgive. I then reminded my friend of this same revelation, and as I have not heard from him since, I hope it has helped him.

Why is it so difficult for most to truly forgive? It seems so difficult to let go of an offence. Being vengeful seems easier and just. Forgiveness only becomes hard because to be vengeful is greedy. To the gracious, forgiveness is simple. It is simple because they have experienced forgiveness from:

> *"so many awful things, I've been cleansed and washed and bathed so many times that when I see a brother who has fallen from the way, I just can't find the license to convict him of his crimes:"*[94]

and pass sentence on another of his crime. This kind of forgiveness can only originate in God. Those who believe

---

[94] Chuck Girard, "Don't Shoot the Wounded," in *Name above all names* (Sea of Glass Music, 1982).

experience it and can then extend the same. Those who do not believe, experience vengeance and extend the same.

The most effective way to become gracious is to experience firsthand, true grace. This grace is none other than the grace of God. Only then can you receive this virtue. For many 'grace' is something you say before a meal.

{ *Parallax: "the apparent displacement of an observed object due to a change in the position of the observer."* }

> *"Grace isn't a little prayer you chant before receiving a meal. It's a way to live." The law tells me how crooked I am. Grace comes along and straightens me out."* (Dwight Lyman Moody).

The greedy believe with conviction that they deserve what they want or have a right to whatever they want. The gracious live in the knowledge that they are completely undeserving of anything good and actually have lost their rights because of the sinful way they have lived. They know the truth of *"for all have sinned and come short of the glory of God," (Rom 3:23)*. The gracious know that 'all' in the above text includes themselves. By this standard, all of mankind are equals.

Copernicus, the great astronomer, directed the following epitaph to be placed on his grave:

> *"O Lord, the faith thou didst give to St. Paul, I cannot ask; the mercy thou didst show to St. Peter, I dare not ask; but, Lord, the grace thou didst show unto the dying robber, that, Lord, show to me."*

This kind of grace is available to all. The following quote was written before the 'N' word was considered discriminatory so do not become focused on its use. See how grace can be seen in its simplest form:

> *"The negro boy down in my Southland years ago, wanted to join a church. So the deacons were examining him. They asked, 'How did you get saved?' His answer was, 'God did His part, and I did my part.' They thought there was something wrong with his doctrine, so they questioned further, 'What was God's part, and what was your part?' His explanation was a good one. He said, 'God's part was the saving, and my part was the sinning. I done run from Him as fast as my sinful heart and rebellious legs could take me. He done took out after me till He run me down.' My friend, that is the way I got saved also."* (J. Vernon McGee, Romans, Vol. 1.)

Perhaps, God is 'done took out after you till He runs you down'. He is chasing you with His grace, not a big stick.

> *"Grace is the central invitation to life and the final word. It's the beckoning nudge and the overwhelming, undeserved mercy that urges us to change and grow, and then gives us the power to pull it off."* (Tim Hansel).

There is no need to run any longer. If you have been a recipient of someone's greed, why continue to be greedy? It need not be so. Accept Gods grace in your life now. Once experienced, you can be transformed. Grace makes one gracious.

Love-P-Self-centeredness

The parallax of love is self-centeredness. The parallax of self-centeredness is love. The person that is pre-occupied with themselves has no room to care for others. If you have love, you have compassion. Self-centeredness has no capacity for compassion, but is curious about the object of loves compassion. The self-centred hoards goods and resources. They are highly attached to things. Love enjoys sharing. Love understands that sacrifice is required and with it, patience. Sacrifice and suffering are intolerable notions to the self-centred, even though these are theirs to experience.

Character	P-Virtue	P-Value	Consequences
• Caring toward others • Compassionate • Shares goods and resources • Sacrificial and patient	Love	Self-centeredness	• Preoccupied with self • Curiosity • Hoards goods and resources • Compromise, Resists sacrifice and suffering

This virtue is about being focused on others. You could almost even place the word 'team' in the place of 'love'. Team, because there is no 'I' in TEAM', nor is there an 'I' in LOVE. Yes, there is no 'I' in SELF-CENTEREDNESS either but there is five 'E's. The value of Self-centeredness is 'all about mE'.

There is a famous band you may have heard of – U2. The lead singer, Bono, was named 'Person of the year' by Time Magazine in 2005, along with Bill and Melinda Gates. Bono is not only known for his music, but also for his work for African aid and economic development. U2 has been together for over 30 years and is considered one of the most successful bands in history. The stereotype of a rock star can be that they are *"self-absorbed, iconoclastic, isolated, and indifferent to others."*[95] This is a stereotype that Bono clearly does not fit into. *"He learned teamwork in the band. Bono recognizes his need for others and, in fact, says he can't imagine having been a solo artist."*[96] I am not sure if it was deliberate, or perhaps prophetic that the band's name is 'U2' rather than 'ME1'.

> *Parallax: "the apparent displacement of an observed object due to a change in the position of the observer."*

Really caring about others

Plenty of people will give a verbal commitment as to how much they care about you, and many have fallen short of that commitment no sooner than when the situation changes. Yet, we still look for someone who really cares, but find ourselves wondering how we will recognize this person as a genuine care giver when we meet them. Another question might be, 'how do I become a person that genuinely cares about another?'

Firstly, it may help to identify the stage that each relationship is in and identify the expectations that align with such a relationship. John Maxwell, in 'Talent is never enough' identifies four stages that relationships go through.

- Stage 1 – Surface – This is the person at the checkout desk, a waiter, or those you recognize from the gym, church, or club. The only expectation here is that these people do what their role requires them to do. It would be unrealistic to say that you care about what kind of day they are having.

---

[95] Maxwell, *Talent is never enough*.
[96] Ibid.

- Stage 2 – Structured – people you meet at routine places or meetings. There is a common interest. All we should care about is if we can start the activity because everyone is there.
- Stage 3 – Secure – trust begins but is fragile and easily broken. There is desire to spend time with each other. This is the friendship level. Some good friends can be made here and there is a low level of caring for another. We also know that good friends can be lost simply by a change in location or circumstance and they are never heard from again.
- Stage 4 – Solid – The friendship survives and builds until full trust and absolute confidentiality exists. There is a desire to serve one another, long term. There is an expectation that the person in your solid relationship has your interests at heart as you do theirs. There is a level of caring here that cannot be broken. *"I feel the capacity to care is the thing which gives life its deepest significance."* (Pablo Casals)

It takes time, possibly years to get to stage 4. There are no shortcuts. Armed with this information, you now know what to believe when a stage 1 relationship person comes up to you and expresses how much they care, or when this person expects from you stage 4 level of caring.

Secondly, to become a person that really cares about others we would be well advised to develop the habit of, as Covey puts it, *"Seek first to understand, then to be understood."*[97]

The person who seeks first to be understood is so pre-occupied with themselves that they couldn't care less about understanding another. I can show that I really do care by listening to you until you are satisfied that I understand you. In order to do this, I have to stop coming up with my set of great answers, formulas and solutions. I literally have to shut down

---

[97] Covey, *The 7 Habits of Highly Effective People*.

my 'biographical' responses. This takes a lot of self discipline as well as great courage. But if I really care, I can do it.

> *"Too often we underestimate the power of a touch, a smile, a kind word, a listening ear, an honest compliment, or the smallest act of caring, all of which have the potential to turn a life around."* (Leo F. Buscaglia)

Compassion

One morning while travelling to work in Sydney as one of thousands exiting central train station, I observed the crowd opening a gap from the top of the stairs and closing again. The gap looked like a circle that was making its way down the stairs directly towards me. When the gap opened in front of me, I discovered the cause. A young girl, in school uniform had fallen backwards at the top of the stairs and came to a stop at the bottom step where I was standing. I wondered why all those people crowded, shoulder to shoulder simply found enough room to step aside and not only let, but watch this girl continue to fall? Curiosity and self-absorption prevented a simple compassionate act from taking place. This is a similar tale of the Good Samaritan found in Luke chapter 10. The curious person is so absorbed in themselves that they experience a temporary blindness to the needs around them and an inability to show or even think of compassion.

Curiosity operates within the framework of judgment. The three elements of judgment are:

1. *"we place ourselves above another as if we were his or her god.*
2. *we condemn another.*
3. *we create the standard for another."*[98]

---

[98] Dr. Henry Cloud, *How People Grow*.

Compassion operates within the framework of evaluation. The three elements of evaluation are:

1. we humble ourselves: *"we identify with a person as a fellow sinner and struggler."*[99]
2. We forgive:*" we do not condemn another person and damn this person with guilt, shame, and wrath of the law. We as sinners are just as guilty and do not have that privilege (Rom2:3)*
3. We correct: *"we do not make up the standard."*[100]

Being curious merely generates interest. Interest only creates questions made up of words. Compassion, on the other hand, motivates into action. It is 'pro-active.' Curiosity will watch a 'dirty job' being performed and be interested in the reason anyone would do such a thing. Compassion sees the need for that 'dirty job' to get done, rolls up its sleeves and does the job. It reminds me of the quote, *"Successful people do the things unsuccessful people don't want to do."* (Origin unknown, claimed by many) In this context the successful person is a compassionate person.

If we look at the compassion in a slightly different way - COME-PASS-UNION, we can derive more meaning. Sometimes when we act in compassion it becomes like grabbing hold of our school girl and falling down the stairs with her. If this takes place, it wasn't compassion, but sympathy. Compassion is like being on a journey and noticing a fellow traveller that has fallen by the way, picking them up and continuing on in the original journey. Come on this journey, through this pass, with me. Not, I will reach out to you and go along this new descending path with you, even for just a while.

"when we see a need, it's good to talk about it, but we must also do something about it."[101]

---

[99] Ibid.
[100] Ibid.

Hoarding – fatal attachments

The partially decomposed rat eaten body of Langley Collyer was found on the 8th of April, 1947, just 10 feet from where the body of his brother, Homer was found 18 days earlier. Langley had died by accidently tripping a booby trap that he had set while crawling through their tunnel made of newspaper, with food for his blind and paralysed brother. The trap released a suitcase and three huge bundles of newspapers, heavy enough to crush Langley. The disabled Homer died some time later, from starvation. His body was found first, and it was after 130 tons of horded things were removed before the grisly and rancid remains of Langley were found. *(See the full story at Collyer brothers - Wikipedia, the free encyclopedia Collyer brothers From Wikipedia, the free encyclopedia)*

This story shows the extreme results that hoarding can have. Today, hoarding is seen as behaviour closely associated with obsessive-compulsive disorder. It is a mental illness, something it seems difficult for the afflicted to admit they have. It is equally difficult for many of us to acknowledge the formation of excessively strong attachments to possessions or even people. There is nothing inherently wrong with being attached to things, unless it comes from the basic value of selfishness.

"Share everything. Don't take things that aren't yours. Put things back where you found them." (Robert Fulghum) Imagine a world like that.

Sacrifice

Successful people are often the people that do the things that the unsuccessful don't do. To do those things, small things, repetitive things, and often unpleasant things involves a sacrifice of the will. It's not that the successful people like

---

[101] "Endures," *Our daily Bread*, no. 2008 (2008).

doing those things. They don't like it. They will bring what they like to do under submission to those things that have to be done.

The Personal Development practitioner sees immediately, from this the meaning of sacrifice, but is it? Tryon Edwards, a Theologian from the 1800's said, *"Compromise is but the sacrifice of one right or good in the hope of retaining another-- too often ending in the loss of both."* It can hardly be considered a sacrifice when you give up something unpleasant in exchange for something better. When we give up something good for something better, we tend to call that a sacrifice. As we see from Tyron Edwards' quote, it is not sacrifice at all. It is really compromise or robbery, and the value that drives compromise is self-centeredness. Mislabelling a compromise as a sacrifice transforms it into a sacrifice about as much as mislabelling a jar of peanut butter turns it into honey. Just because you are wearing the uniform, doesn't make you a fireman.

It seems to me that sacrifice has been mislabelled for hundreds of years and by many. Charles Du Bos said, *""The important thing is this: To be able at any moment to **sacrifice** what we are for what we could become."* The creator of Peter Pan, James Matthew Barrie wrote, *"Dreams do come true, if we only wish hard enough. You can have anything in life if you will sacrifice everything else for it."* These quotes, on the surface sound great, but the sacrifice will only be made in order to serve self. For Mr Du Bos, the 'important thing' is the becoming of self. For Mr Barrie, its having for oneself, anything.

The deeper meaning of sacrifice is the giving up of something good, great or better – full stop. I was reminded of this in a discussion with a friend who was in the middle of a 'fast'. A 'fast' can be otherwise defined as a sacrifice of food or behaviour. My friend was considering breaking her fast early because she felt she had received what she was fasting for. On further inquiry, I found she had indeed received something during the time of that fast, but what she received was not related to the original reason for fasting. The original reason for fasting was to support a friend in their fast. It was like a light was just turned on. The original fast was totally devoid of selfishness. It was totally 'other-centred'. Nothing was expected in return, and so there was no reason to break the fast.

If the meaning of true sacrifice expects nothing in return, common sense should prevail when it comes to what to sacrifice. *"The greatest of follies is to sacrifice health for any other kind of happiness."* (Arthur Schopenhauer, German Philosopher, 1788-1860) To, by virtue, truly sacrifice something, one must consider it gone and utterly forever lost, and for the sake of others.

When compromises are made, even in the name of sacrifice the failure to become 'a greater and better humanity' will be inevitably possible, and will have to be tolerated.

> *"It is not tolerable, it is not possible, that from so much death, so much sacrifice and ruin, so much heroism, a greater and better humanity shall not emerge."* (Charles de Gaulle, French general, writer and statesman, 1890-1970)

The greatest sacrifice of life for love of others, more specifically, you and I, was that of the Lord Jesus Christ. He did so on the cross and forgave all the sins (past/present/future) of the world. How great a love is this that gives its life for you and me without the guarantee that all would respond and believe in Him?

Servant-hood P Significance

The parallax of servant-hood is significance. A sense of needed significance can look like service. Looking like something doesn't mean that something is that thing. The parallax of significance is servant-hood. Being of service, no matter the size, is significant.

Character	P-Virtue	P-Value	Consequences
<ul><li>Uses position to enhance and advance others</li><li>Attentive to others' needs</li><li>Seeks to serve others</li><li>Views resources as means of helping others</li></ul>	Servant-hood	Significance	<ul><li>Seeks noticeable and affirmed significance</li><li>Insensitive to others' needs</li><li>Expects others to serve</li><li>Materialistic</li></ul>

My friend (I will call Charlie Brown) will wonder why I tell this story, if he recognises himself. He would probably prefer I did not tell it. Sorry Charlie (not his real name), but you are the best example I can think of to commence this chapter. I tell it because when I think of a person that best reflects a virtue of servant-hood, I think of Charlie Brown (my friend, not the cartoon character). He is the CEO of company that distributes Bibles. It is one of the bigger companies that provide this service and part of his remuneration package is a company car. The allowance is enough to purchase a car in the luxury range. If Charlie Brown was the kind of person who was seeking significance, he would have used all he was allocated and be showing me his Audi, Merc or BM. That's not Charlie

> *Parallax: "the apparent displacement of an observed object due to a change in the position of the observer."*

though. He purchases a car that meets his needs at the best value, which is substantially less than what was allocated. Even then, you would have to be talking him into getting a company car rather than drive his own. You would probably need to ask Charlie the reason, but from where I sit, I see a man who just wants to serve his God, which has placed him in position where he can do this best. His attitude is one of service and it is reflected in all his business choices. The left over money for the car can put hundreds of Bibles into the hands of those who need it.

Position

A position can be an actual job title or a 'positioning' of ourselves. It can be seen as a means of being noticed or appearing significant, or a means advancing others.

It seems that Henry Rollins was trying to use his position to get others started when he said, *"This is my 25th year of being on stage. A lot of people who I kind of toed up to the starting line with are no longer in this position. I feel very, very lucky."*

Position brings with it power. Power is amoral, until someone gets a hold of it. John Adams wrote:

> *"Because power corrupts, society's demands for moral authority and character increase as the importance of the position increases."*

Power as a virtue, or a value is determined by the character driver of that person. *"Power does not corrupt men; fools, however, if they get into a position of power, corrupt power."* (George Bernard Shaw)

For the significance seeker, position feeds the ego. Colin Powell wisely said, *" Don't let your ego get too close to your position, so that if your position gets shot down, your ego doesn't go with it."* For the servant, position is merely a means to increase service capacity. The ego is not invested. Should the position get 'shot down', the servant merely seeks out another means to serve.

Service is 'other-centred'. Significance is 'self-centred'. Significance is similar to, or can manifest itself by a desire to be fascinating. Katharine Hepburn said, *"Trying to be fascinating is an asinine[102] position to be in."* The 'other-centred' person works to not attract attention to their position.

Attentive or insensitive

Those seeking significant are self-centred. Children are also often self-centred. Self-centred, in a way, that they have not developed an awareness of their surroundings. That awareness comes as they grow up and become mature. Seeking significance can also be immature. To be attentive requires maturity. Julius Gordon writes:

> *"How do we know that Moses was grown up? Because he went out unto his brethren, and was ready to bear the burdens and share the plight of his people. Maturity is sensitivity to human suffering."*

Maturity is sensitive, or attentive, or even aware of the surroundings. Replacing the word sensitivity with attentiveness serves our purpose better here. Immaturity is insensitivity to the point of inattentiveness to human activity around you.

Awareness is influenced by the virtue, or the value that motivates. Before we discuss this, let's go back to the use of the word attentive, rather than sensitive. A seemingly strange admission from the boxing Champion, Mike Tyson is, *"My biggest weakness is my sensitivity. I am too sensitive a person."* Being attentive is a proactive character trait. Proactive character traits are strengths. Being sensitive or insensitive is a

---

[102] Asinine: foolish, unintelligent, or silly; stupid; it is surprising that supposedly intelligent people can make such asinine statements. Of or like an ass; asinine obstinacy; asinine features

consequence, a reaction. Being reactive is a weakness. *"Wallow too much in sensitivity and you can't deal with life, or the truth."* (Neal Boortz)

Significance driven people are 'all about themselves'. *"But I think that sensitivity is also a good counselor*[sic] *when it comes to enforcing one's interests."* (Johannes Rau) And that is about as far as they can see. The boundaries of their awareness are marked clearly around what they consider to be their interests or space. The servant-hood driven person is 'all about everyone else' and that determines the boundaries of their awareness.

{ *Parallax: "the apparent displacement of an observed object due to a change in the position of the observer."* }

I am a surviving biker from about 30 years ago. The reason I say 'surviving' is because my sense of awareness to my surroundings whilst riding my customized Kawasaki, was acute keeping me alive. The motorbike itself is not dangerous. It's all the other road users, particularly the ones that thought it was okay to 'under-take' me on a narrow country road. A road used mostly by coal trucks. The part of the road where this happened was on approaching a turning crest, with double centre lines. If I was too wrapped up in how I looked on my shiny bike (significance) I would not have been aware of the driver's intentions of performing this dangerous manoeuvre, which in turn would have added the element of surprise, potentially resulting in an accident. I did sense the need to make the driver attentive (service) to my rightful presence on the road by re-shaping his door with an imprint of my steel-capped boot as he passed me.

Service or expect

When I was in my first year of Bible College (the steel-capped boot incident happened before this), I was serving in my local church as a practical component of the course I was doing. I almost failed, because the report sent back to the Dean stated that I refused to serve. This was one of those 'please explain' meetings. What had taken place was the receptionist at the church had taken it upon herself to determine that I, the lower person on the food chain, Bible College student, needed a lesson in servant-hood and proceeded to order me in to clean the toilets. The report to the Dean contained my refusal to comply. I needed to attempt an explanation which went something like this; 'I don't like cleaning toilets, but there is no problem in doing this 'dirty job' if I see the need for it to be done. In this case, they didn't need cleaning and I thought it was obvious, by the tone used, that the only reason I was being asked to do it was so the receptionist could rejoice in her ability to control another (man in particular) and get a feeling of significance from it.'

The virtue of servant-hood discovers a need and realizes that because he has discovered it, it can only mean that he is the answer and serves to meet the need. The value of significance also discovers the need, but looks for someone else to meet the need, whilst taking the credit for the needs discovery.

As this receptionist was there to serve also, I felt her request was inappropriate, but only equal to my inappropriate response when I told her to do it herself. After all, she was the servant that discovered the need.

The point is that sometimes the difference between seeking to serve others and expecting others to serve can be subtle. Albert Einstein said, *"The road to perdition has ever been accompanied by lip service to an ideal."* Often the significant appears to be a servant, but in the end it is only lip service. Robert Frost puts another slant on it, *"Pressed into service means pressed out of shape."*

Service from a value driven person is really administered so that others will be expected to serve likewise. Service from a virtuous person is pure service, absent of reciprocation or expectation. Mohandas Gandhi said, *"That service is the noblest which is rendered for its own sake."*

It is not what we are called [significance], but what we do [serve] that counts. The most significant people at a wedding are, understandably the bride and groom. But here is an example of servant-hood as opposed to significance. On this wedding day, instead of holding a grand reception for the newlyweds, it was decided to provide a feast for the homeless using the church yard as the venue[103]. This idea could only come from a servant's heart. This idea is also not unique. See the story of a wedding in the Gospel of Luke chapter 14:7-14[104]. The servant asks what he can put into the lives of others. The significant asks what he can get out of life.

When the focus is on what we get rather than what we give, productivity and accomplishment plummets. It has been said, *"It is amazing what can be accomplished when we don't care*

---

[103] Anne Cetas, "Serving Together," *Our daily Bread*, no. June, July, August 2008 (2008).

[104] And He put forth a parable to those who were invited, when He noted how they chose out the chief places, saying to them, When you are invited by anyone to a wedding, do not recline in the chief seat, lest a more honorable *man* than you may be invited by him. And he who invited you and him shall come and say to you, Give place to this man; and then you begin with shame to take the last place. But when you are invited, go and recline in the lowest place, so that when he who invited you comes, he may say to you, Friend, go up higher. Then glory shall be to you before those reclining with you. For whoever exalts himself shall be abased, and he who humbles himself shall be exalted. And He also said to him who invited Him, When you make a dinner or a supper, do not call your friends or your brothers, or your kinsmen, or *your* rich neighbors; lest they also invite you again, and a recompense be made to you. But when you make a feast, call the poor, the maimed, the lame, the blind, and you shall be blessed, for they cannot repay you; for you shall be repaid at the resurrection of the just. And one of those who reclined with *Him* heard these things, and *he* said to Him, Blessed *are* those eating bread in the kingdom of God. (Luk 14:7-15)

who gets the credit."[105] It is equally amazing how little gets accomplished when all we want is all the credit.

Who is it that most often expects others to serve? Usually these are office-holders or a person who holds a 'position' in an organization, or otherwise known as leaders. Max De Pree, is possibly best known as a leader from this quote: *"the first responsibility of a leader is to define reality."* This was immediately followed by the following;

> *"The last is to say thank you. In between the two, the leader must become a servant and a debtor. That sums up the progress of an artful leader."*[106]

Expecting others to serve is really another way of trying to control others. *"True strength comes when we stop trying to control people and start serving them instead."*[107] The seeking of significance is a reflection of the loss of self. *"The best way to find yourself is to lose yourself in the service of others."* (Mohandas Gandhi)

Only the significant have a reputation. Those who serve have character, which may lead into a significant reputation. *"If we take care of our character, our reputation will take care of itself."*[108] To have reputation [significance] without character [servant] is short-lived success. To possess a reputation that has developed from a strong character makes this person a 'jewel of the kingdom'.

---

[105] Bill Crowder, "The Richness of Humility," *Our daily Bread*, no. March, April, May 2008 (2008).
[106] Dave Branon, "The Debt of Leadership," *Our daily Bread*, no. March, April, May 2008 (2008).
[107] Julie Ackerman Link, "Strength in Weakness," *Our daily Bread*, no. December, January, Febuary 2009-2010 (2010).
[108] Julie Ackerman Link, "Bribery," *Our daily Bread*, no. June, July, August 2010 (2010).

> *"The general who advances without coveting fame and retreats without fearing disgrace, whose only thought is to protect his country and do good service for his sovereign, is the jewel of the kingdom."* (Sun Tzu)

Resources/Materialism

Everyone knows part or some variation of this Bible verse, *"For the love of money is a root of all evils, of which some having lusted after, they were seduced from the faith and pierced themselves through with many sorrows."* (1Ti 6:10)

Property, whether physical or intellectual, is amoral. Whether they become material or resource is determined by the virtue/value of the possessor.

To the significant, everything is material: materials to be sought after, to satisfy one's own selfish needs. Materials can be things, like a car, a house, a stereo or any of millions of products. People, with their skills and talents, are often seen as materials to the seeker of significance.

To the servant, everything is a resource, inclusive of skills and talents. When the servant receives some materials there first thought is how to economically utilize this resource for those whom he serves. The Basket ball player Kareem Abdul-Jabbar said, *"I can do something else besides stuff a ball through a hoop. My biggest resource is my mind."*

This subtle difference between material and resources might help to explain this 'why':

> *"It seems that almost every time a valuable natural resource is discovered in the world-whether it be diamonds, rubber, gold, oil, whatever-often what results is a tragedy for the country in which they are found. Making matters worse, the resulting riches from these resources rarely benefit the people of the country from which they come.* (Edward Zwick)

Let's cut right to the chase of significance and service. The real bottom line issue here is pride or humility.

Motivation

The 'great' carrot and stick motivation technique is used in many workplaces today, and illustrated by a man sitting on a donkey with a fishing pole in one hand (a carrot in front of the donkeys nose) and a stick in the other hand, aimed at the donkeys rear-end. But, it only works for the person seeking significance and at best yields temporary results, requiring a further repeated application of the technique.

For the person who is really a servant, this motivation technique is better known as the great jack-ass theory. Meaning, you would have to be a jack-ass to fall for it.

At first the donkey will attempt to get the carrot. He becomes frustrated because the carrot (the goal post) keeps moving forward with every step taken. Progress, however is being made, for the time being. Should the donkey tire of the ever moving goal post, he will lose interest in progress and the carrot. He will stop, only to find the pain inflicted by the stick makes him move again.

In the very rare case of the donkey being more intelligent – he will turn and bite the rider on the leg, or buck him off all together. Who is the Jack-Ass now?

Jesus has been called the servant king. A short study of His life will reveal that punishment (the whip) and/or reward (the carrot) failed to motivate Him. Serving His God given purpose provided lasting and unquenchable motivation.

For those with a 'significant mindset' (in danger of becoming jack-asses) yesterdays' failures can bankrupt tomorrow's efforts. You may remember the story of Peter, one of Jesus' closest disciples. Peter considered himself to be significant in serving the Lord and openly claimed he would never abandon or deny Jesus. Yet, he did this very thing, three times. Oh, the depths that the significant fall to when they fall. Peter felt so bad and considered all his dreams smashed, he went back to his old trade – fishing. We pick up the story in John 21 where after fishing he returns to land to find the resurrected Jesus waiting for him by a fire. He was waiting for Peter to call him back into service. Because Jesus forgives our failures, the servant is free to best utilise tomorrows efforts by servicing in a significant way.

Going from significant to servant requires more than reformation or self-development. It requires a parallax: regeneration.

Acts of service, small or great, are all important.

Small acts of service should never be underestimated for the results can grow.

> "Edward Kimball a Sunday school teacher in Boston, decided to visit a young man in his class...that day he led that man Dwight L. Moody to the Lord...had a major impact on Wilbur Chapman...a prominent evangelist, recruited Billy Sunday who...invited Mordecai Ham... in one of those meetings, Billy Graham received Christ as his Saviour..."[109]

The difference between significance and service is what we are 'called' and what we 'do.' What we do (serve) is what counts.

---

[109] Joe Stowell, "Small things," *Our daily Bread*, no. March April May (2011).

> "...man has tried to distinguish himself through monuments of all kinds...it is a fact of life that every monumental work will likely be surpassed...man's biggest 'successes' are fleeting. Our best efforts bring temporary honor[sic], which all too soon will be eclipsed by the new and greater achievements of others..."[110]

In the world without God it is often thought that significance needs to come before service can be of any value. Arnold Schwarzenegger is one of many examples on display when he said:

> "I didn't leave bodybuilding until I felt that I had gone as far as I could go. It will be the same with my film career. When I feel the time is right, I will then consider public service. I feel that the highest honor[sic] comes from serving people and your country." (Arnold Schwarzenegger)

But it is not the case.

> "As far as service goes, it can take the form of a million things. To do service, you don't have to be a doctor working in the slums for free, or become a social worker. Your position in life and what you do doesn't matter as much as how you do what you do." (Elisabeth Kubler-Ross)

If we don't learn to serve, we cannot become significant. We don't need to be significant in order to serve.

> "But Jesus called them and said to them, You know that they who are accounted rulers over the nations exercise lordship over them. And their great ones exercise authority on them. But it shall not be so among you. But

---

[110] C. P. Hia, "Building a city," *Our daily Bread* September October November(2008).

whoever desires to be great among you, let him be your servant." (Mar 10:42-43)

> *"True greatness does not lie with those*
> *who strive for worldly fame:*
> *it lies instead with those who choose*
> *to serve in Jesus' name."*[111]

---

[111] D. De Haan, "Building a City," *Our daily Bread* September October November(2008).

Humility- P- Pride

The parallax of humility is pride. It is possible to be proud of humility, but humility cannot be proud of it. The parallax of pride is humility.

Character	P-Virtue	P-Value	Consequences
<ul><li>Gives credit where due</li><li>Accepts assigned place</li><li>Obedient</li><li>Grateful.</li></ul>	Humility	Pride	<ul><li>Takes credit to self</li><li>Envious, jealous</li><li>Arrogant, assertive</li><li>Insubordinate, grumbling.</li></ul>

The virtue of humility *"is a choice, not a state of being."*[112] It is a conscious choice. Pride also is a choice, not a state of being. It is however a choice by default because of the presence of the 'old sin nature' which all humans are born with, when the choice of humility is not made. Some would not choose humility over pride because the humble person is often seen as a person that is *"quiet, unassuming, undemanding, frail, and easily victimized and carry all this with a kind and sweet spirit."*[113] Some of these qualities are somewhat attractive, while most are not. So if that is what it means to be humble, many would choose pride. What if the perceived definition of the humble is incorrect?

> *"It would be possible for someone to be rather bold, courageous, clearly articulate, and highly effective and at the same time manifest a true spirit of humility. In fact, isn't that an exact profile of our King?"*[114]

---

[112] Stowell, *Eternity: Reclaiming a passion for what endures*.
[113] Ibid.
[114] Ibid.

By 'our King' Stowell is referring to Jesus Christ. If you don't know Him like this, reading one of the four recognized biographical works, otherwise known as the Gospels might help. The Gospel of John would be a good place to start.

True humility is not only a choice, but two choices:

1. *"A choice to recognize that all we are and all we accomplish is due only to the fact that Someone else has made it possible for us to succeed."*[115] This reminds me again of the story of the turtle found sitting on a fence-post. He achieved great heights, but he had to have help. To make this choice also means to sacrifice any self-credit due. That struggle you may be feeling now is called pride.
2. *"Chooses to humble its will in submission to a higher moral authority."*[116] To make this choice is to admit that 'it's not all about you.' Or 'you don't know it all or even what is best.' In fact, in the whole collection of all knowledge, you don't know anything. Nor do I. This may be difficult to admit, particularly for the teenager who woke up one morning and knows everything. Even more difficult, for the one who has spent the majority of his or her life maintaining this obviously false belief. Once contemplated, it is a rather mean trick to play on them by letting them go on believing it.

This 'know it all' mentality can get people into a lot of trouble or on a lighter level, provide a great deal of hilarity. I recall coming home to find a guest attempting to tune my guitar. She claimed that there was something wrong with my guitar and it could not be tuned. There is a couple of things my reader needs to know at this point: a] my guest is a blonde, b] my guest is right handed, c] my guest considers herself a self-taught expert on the guitar, and d] I am left-handed and so is my guitar.

---

[115] Ibid.
[116] Ibid.

Giving or Taking Credit

What is truly in the heart of man will determine whether he gives credit or takes credit. Humility or pride; it will be one or the other. There is one word that encompasses both the virtue and the value – self-esteem. There is a great body of literary works just on this subject. Indeed, the first book I ever read from cover to cover was titled 'Self-love'. There is another book considered famous by many called 'I'm okay, you're okay'. It is on my shelf, though I have not read it, and therefore cannot even begin to form an opinion on the content, nor is it my intention to do so here. I was simply reminded of this title when I read from 'The Revolution of the Character':

> *"Our initial move towards Christ-likeness cannot be toward self-esteem. Realistically, I'm not okay, and you're not okay. We're all in serious trouble.... Self-esteem in our situation will only breed self-deception and frustration."*[117]

The proud will demand credit. After all, he is worth it and deserves it. But is this reality or an illusion? A superiority complex is usually an inferiority complex in disguise.

The humble gives credit away so freely that he often includes what is rightfully his in that gift. There is something he knows in his heart about whom he really is and that without God, he is nothing, worthless and incapable of being independent in any way. In fact, it is God who determines ones worth. The following text describes what God does to the proud and just to make you curious, it's about Jeremiahs underwear.

> *"So says Jehovah to me, Go and buy for yourself a linen girdle, and put it on your loins, and do not put it in*

---

[117] Don Simpson Dallas Willard, *Revolution of Character* (Nottingham: Inter-Varsity Press, 2006).

water. *(2) So I bought a girdle according to the Word of Jehovah, and put it on my loins. (3) And the Word of Jehovah came to me a second time, saying, (4) Take the girdle that you bought, which is on your loins, and arise. Go to Euphrates, and hide it there in a hole of the rock. (5) So I went and hid it by Euphrates, as Jehovah commanded me. (6) And it happened at the end of many days Jehovah said to me, Arise, go to Euphrates and take the girdle from there, which I commanded you to hide there. (7) Then I went to Euphrates and dug, and took the girdle from the place where I had hidden it.* **And, behold, the girdle was rotted; it was not good for anything.** *(8) Then the Word of Jehovah came to me, saying, (9) So* **says Jehovah, In this way I will spoil the pride of Judah and the great pride of Jerusalem. (10) This evil people, who refuse to hear My Words, who walk in the stubbornness of their heart and walk after other gods to serve them and to worship them, shall even be like this girdle, which is good for nothing.** *(11) For as the girdle holds fast to the loins of a man, so I have caused the whole house of Israel and the whole house of Judah to cling to Me, says Jehovah; so that they might be to Me for a people, and for a name, and for a praise, and for a glory; but they would not hear."* (Jer.13:1-11)

Be put In Your Place

Where there is a will, there is a way. It isn't always true though.

Only the proud will not accept anything or any place less than what they want. They see what another has and decide that they too should not only have it, but have more. Enter the dynamic duo of motivators: envy and jealousy.

The humble are able to accept where they are and what they have. That is not to say that they don't aim at arrival to a better place or acquiring better things. They just aren't driven to it.

There is something else the humble person knows about his heart. It is not about 'my' will be done; it is about 'His' will be done. Without God, mans will only has the power at best to make a copy. Where there is a will, there is a way, but it is not 'The Way'. The statement is actually from a proud life.

The human will does have some power though, especially if it is fuelled with pride. This next story remains a mystery, but it illustrates the 'I know what I am doing' mentality. I came home one day to find our VCR player[118] broken. The 'eject' button had disappeared somewhere in the unit. What had happened was clear. When the button was pushed, causing an electrical circuit to connect, the video was supposed to eject. In this case, it didn't work so; the second strategy was to press harder, as though it had some kind of mechanical leverage system under it. The machine has been broken ever since. The mystery is who did it? I suppose pride prevents admission.

Obedient or Arrogant

I recall a story about a boy who was in trouble. His father sent him to the chair in the corner. He initially refused to sit. After the father exercised his authority, the boy sat down in obedience but said, 'I might be sitting on the outside, but I am still standing on the inside.' I think if my children ever said that, I would have trouble not laughing, even on the inside. The truth in this story is obedience is not always obedience. The reader may have seen a grown up version: known as the 'yes man'. Obedience is not blind, especially when it comes to those who just happen to be in a place of authority. The 'yes man' person is obedient on the outside, but something else on the inside. We call that arrogance.

True obedience can only come from humility. From the one who has made the second choice: *"Chooses to humble his will*

---

[118] For those accustomed to DVD's and Blue-ray players, a VCR is a video player. Ask your grandparents to show you what a video looks like.

in submission to a higher moral authority."[119] It would be considered wise as to whom that higher moral authority is. To elevate a human to that role might really be a contribution to the 'pride-fest'[120]

Grateful – All I Need Is The Air That I Breath

The self-appointed 'deserving' person, by definition is a needy person, will find it difficult to be grateful when they receive any gift. The needy person thinks they deserve. Somebody out there owes them a living. They can only come to this conclusion if they think of themselves more highly than they ought. (Rom.12:3) We call that pride.

The humble is grateful for even the air they breathe. Grateful that they can breathe it while they slept last night and grateful that they woke up and am now breathing. Anything else

> *Parallax: "the apparent displacement of an observed object due to a change in the position of the observer."*

they get is a bonus and even more reason to be grateful. This is not descriptive of a person trying to look humble by refusing gifts or rewards. The humble gratefully accept whatever they are given, and there is a genuineness about them. I sometimes wonder how long it would take for pride to dissipate and humble gratitude to be acknowledged if you put all the proud ungrateful people in a sealed room and sucked all the air out of it.

Only the humble are teachable. The proud, or the arrogant think they know it all and because of that thinking, cannot be taught.

> *"Strength of Character and resultant happiness are constructed upon a foundation of humility. Humility is freedom – freedom from subjectivity – allowing you to*

---

[119] Stowell, *Eternity: Reclaiming a passion for what endures*.
[120] PRIDE-FEST: a gathering where everyone strokes the ego's of each other so they can all feel good and important.

comprehend objective reality... Humility is the basic human virtue of teachability"[121]

The humble are also recipients of Gods graces, while the proud and arrogant are recipients of Gods warfare (Prov. 3:33-35; Jam.4:6; 1Pet. 5:5-6)

The humble *"acknowledges his weaknesses and depends on a strength greater than his own,"* while the *"arrogant person places himself in a position of weakness by overestimating his strengths. He can neither think rationally nor make wise decisions,..."*[122].

Humility is the mindset or disposition believers are commanded to adopt just as Christ was disposed to. Phil.2: 2-11.

"then fulfill my joy, that you may be like-minded, having the same love, being of one accord and of one mind. (3) Let nothing be done through strife or vainglory, but in lowliness of mind let each esteem others better than themselves. (4) Do not let each man look upon his own things, but each man also on the things of others. (5) For let this mind be in you which was also in Christ Jesus, (6) who, being in the form of God, thought it not robbery to be equal with God, (7) but made Himself of no reputation, and took upon Himself the form of a servant, and was made in the likeness of men. (8) And being found in fashion as a man, He humbled Himself and became obedient unto death, even the death of the cross. (9) Therefore God has highly exalted Him, and has given Him a name which is above every name, (10) that at the name of Jesus every knee should bow, of heavenly ones, and of earthly ones, and of ones under the earth; (11) and that every tongue should confess that Jesus Christ is Lord, to the glory of God the Father." (Php 2:2-11)

---

[121] R. B. Thieme, *Christian Integrity*: 65.
[122] Ibid., 67.

Justice-P-Oppression

The parallax of Justice is oppression. The opposite is injustice. The parallax of oppression is justice. The opposite is freedom.

Character	P-Virtue	P- Value	Consequences
• Seeks to relieve the oppressed • Protects others • Promotes equality of mankind .	Justice	Oppression	• Victimised weak for personal gain • Ruins others to enhance self • Promotes racial/ethnic strife.

There is only One that is able to apply justice because He is Just. That however, doesn't stop, nor should it stop us from working for justice.

> "...but Scripture promises that God will one day avenge all injustices (Rom.12:19). While we wait, we are to do what we can to work for justice and leave the results in God's hands."[123]

Of course if there is no God included, there is only the decision to take the results into our own hands. In a word – revenge. This only leads to oppression. In short, justice is a virtue attainable from the only One who has it. So any denial of God places this virtue out of reach. Funny thing about this is that the Personal Development practitioner who denies God will still fight for the attainment of this virtue, and the more they fight, the more oppression results. One of the Bibles well known quotes is 'we will know them by their fruits.' That comes from Matthew 7:16 and again in verse 20. The fruit or consequences of the oppressor are victims, ruined people and racial/ethical strife.

---

[123] Julie Ackerman Link, "Poetic Justice," *Our daily Bread*, no. September, October, November 2011 (2011).

The fruit or character of the just is relief or rescuing from victimisation, protects others and promotes equality.

Victims

Victims are the result of people being treated as commodities. When people are seen or viewed as commodities, a polite way of saying they are there to be used for another's gain, oppression has been active. Our most blatant example of this is the slave trade. We however have more subtle examples in our society. A more relatable example would be the employer/employee relationship. Is it not true that as soon as an employee's services are no longer required his position disappears and he is retrenched? Yes, out of a sense of trying to be just, they are often retrained or moved to another position, which happens to be closer to the door. It is perhaps harsh to put it like this but the employer/employee system has similarities to the master/slave system. By the way, this was one of the first things I learnt in a Human Resource Management course I did. Just ask who always draws the short straw, or gets the rough end of the stick. Doesn't this describe the oppressor/victim system being discussed here?

Christopher J. McCullough, published a book in 1995 titled 'Nobodies victim.' It is in my opinion one of the greatest book written on the subject of effective counselling and therapy, but anyone searching for this book will be met with some difficulty. The situation which describes why it is hard to find is both ironic and unfair, or unjust. The author sent the book off to be published and that was the last he heard or saw of it. That is, until I wrote a review on Amazon.com. I received an email from the author who thanked me for my comments and asked how I came to be in possession of this 'lost book'. I had picked it up at one of those discount book stalls in Sydney and paid $2.50 for it. On Dr. McCullough's request, I returned to the book stall and purchased all remaining copies (about 20) and mailed them to him in the US. The irony is in the loss of a book with such a title and justice is yet to be served regarding the contribution that this book makes. I will try to implement some justice by using it as a major source document describing this area of victim-hood.

Dr. McCullough writes:

> *"victimhood...is not the natural consequence of abuse. It is our attitude toward the abuse that determines whether or not we feel like a victim"*[124] (Inside jacket)

and then:

> *"But cause, in itself, does not define victimhood; blame does. Blame and victimhood say, 'you have taken something from me and I can't feel good about myself until you confess and repent.'"*[125]

Blame says, 'it's your fault' or 'it's not fair.' Blame is a seeking of justice, but it never leads to it. Blame determines that a person has become a victim and as such the only 'just' thing to do is oppress the object of the blaming to achieve any sense of justice.

{ *Parallax: "the apparent displacement of an observed object due to a change in the position of the observer."* }

Once a victim, it is not always a victim. Change can happen and part of that change has to do with the acknowledgement and then the willingness to lose the benefits of being a victim. Yes, that's right! There are benefits to being a victim. For more information see Dr Phil's book on Life Strategies. Especially the chapter that discusses what the 'pay-off' is. Being a victim offers:

---

[124] Christopher J. McCullough, *Nobodies Victim* (New York: Clarkson Potter/Publishers, 1995). Inside front jacket.
[125] Ibid.

> "1. Victims receive care and attention. 2. The victim's own destructive behaviour is obscured. 3. Victims are justified in not exercising their responsibilities. 4. Victims may feel power over their abusers. 5. Victimhood can help you avoid dealing with other fundamental issues of life. 6. Victims can share a feeling of belonging and connection. 7. Wearing the badge of victimhood creates a sense of identity where one is missing."[126]

The victim must also learn to;

> "move beyond blame-laying or pathologizing our symptoms of unhappiness, we must learn to stop finding the reason for our pain and focus instead on facing it head on. Here are a few suggestions. 1. Accept that bad things will happen in your life...2. Admit to yourself that you don't control everything that happens to you... 3. Recognize that pain and suffering can be a natural evolution stage. The fact is that pain, once it's accepted, propels us into movement. Notice I did not say, 'pain is a growth experience' or 'pain helps us change'. I'm not convinced that most of us would seek change and growth if pain and suffering were the price."... 'Pain is pain – a simple painful fact... suffering, however, is only and always the refusal of pain, the claim that life should not be painful; it is the rejection of a fact, the denial of life and of the nature of things... 4. Allow others to see you suffering."[127]

Just as;

> "you partake of treatment but are never fulfilled, because 'help' programs offer only a cheap substitute for what is missing in your life. Therapy and support

---

[126] Ibid., 12-13.
[127] Ibid.

> *groups cannot replace true community; hired empathisers can never serve as well as caring family members and friends."* [128]

This is not to different to what the Bible describes as a 'hireling':

> *"But he who is a hireling and not the shepherd, who does not own the sheep, sees the wolf coming and leaves the sheep and runs away. And the wolf catches them and scatters the sheep. The hireling flees, because he is a hireling and does not care for the sheep."* (Joh 10:12-13)

Developing the character trait of oppressor is a cheap substitute for the virtue of justice. Character cannot replace virtue.

Apple Pie mentality

The next consequence of oppression I call the Apple Pie mentality. It describes how we often think, an outlook or point of view. Once a piece of the pie has been taken, there is less for everyone else. As more pieces are taken, the realisation comes that if you are not quick enough, you won't get your piece of pie. As desperation sets in you take what you can get, not caring who you step on or push-in on. It reminds me of a local supermarket that has sales on every Thursday. At least an hour before opening time the line of adults is pushing and shoving to be the first in. They don't want to miss out. As the store attendant starts to open the door a mass weight of a lot of desperate people begin to push. Children are trampled, the elderly are pushed aside and there is much colourful language to be heard.

'Press' is in the middle of op'press'ion. The same sort of thing happens at those 'end of financial year' sales. I must be honest here, I really don't relate to these situations as I have only been

---

[128] Ibid., 27.

an observer from a safe distance. To bring the point closer to home is there anyone in your household that picks off the favourite topping off the pizza before anyone can get a slice? If it does happen in your home, check the crazed desperate look in their eyes before protesting. It could be hazardous to your health and safety to interfere. Once upon a time I had two dogs, both with powerful jaws and both protective of their food. A fight broke out and I made the error of reaching my hand in to intervene. I will leave it up to your imagination to figure out what happened next.

On a more serious note, a common discussion takes place with the three to four year old when they feel neglected due to the arrival of their baby sister. The toddler has already developed the idea that a parents love is like a pie. Now that there are more kids to love, they must love them less.

So we can trace this mentality to being a toddler where the consequences are relatively small. Carry that same mentality through to adulthood and the consequences can be devastating. Now people are prepared to ruin others to enhance self. The end (all-important-self) justifies the means (ruin of others).

The character trait of oppression will defend itself with little or no regard for the well being or safety of others. The virtue of justice seeks to protect others, even at the cost of self-defence. It is selfless, rather than selfish.

Racism

Racism is another result of oppression. Other words that come to mind with racism are prejudice, favouritism, discrimination, stereotyping, respect and freedom. Australia is a multicultural and multi-socioeconomically class country that has its share of racial and anti-discrimination legislation to try and live together in a peaceful fashion. Everyone in Australia knows about 'equal opportunity' and the majority have the intention to live by it and treat people with equality. The fairness and justice that these articles of legislation are designed to produce are not too difficult to see. In practice, however, it is often another matter.

Those that live on the north shore of Sydney are often stereotyped as wealthy in comparison to perhaps those living in Sydney's far west. Though many offensive names for those from other countries have almost been eliminated (we had a biscuit called 'Gollywogs' and it has been changed to 'Scallywags'), it seems the object of those name-calling have the exclusive right to call themselves by that name. For example, an Italian may excuse being called a 'wog' if he uses this term when referring to himself. I called someone that when I was in high school, I am ashamed to say, and ended up in a fist fight, which I lost, and deservedly so.

We still have areas where a game is played, in the privacy of our vehicles, called 'spot the Aussie'. Then there are plenty of examples of those who were the target of racism, now protected by law, carry out racist acts on Australians. It's all getting murky.

I am reminded of another story, a fictitious one, told about a school bus driver way out in outback Australia. His passengers consisted of Australian kids and native Australian kids. They would fight each other every day on the way to and from school. Finally, exasperated by the situation, the driver stopped the bus in the middle of nowhere and ordered everyone off. He lined them up and gave a great lecture on how he would not tolerate such behaviour anymore. He had a solution and he explained how whenever anyone gets on his bus, they will suddenly be one colour – green. Just to be sure the kids understood he asked one of the Australian kids, 'what colour are you?' The reply was, 'green sir.' Turning to one of the native Australians, he asked the same question. Again the response was 'green sir.' Satisfied that he was understood, the driver ordered the kids back on the bus with the following instructions, 'the light green can sit on the right and the dark green can sit on the left.'

As much as we try, there is a ring of truth to *"in the world, diversity divides, in the church diversity unites."*[129] At least that is the way it is supposed to be. The Apostle Paul wrote a great deal about this issue because the Jewish Christians were basically racist against the Greek Christians and vice-versa. He wrote:

> *"There cannot be Jew nor Greek, there is neither bond nor free, there is no male nor female; for you are all one in Christ Jesus."* (Gal 3:28).

The answer to finding justice in this area is not in legislation, for values held by individuals cannot be legislated. It's like trying to make people ascribe to a faith, by law, for living in a particular country. Once again, we can conclude that the only place justice can be found in this area is in Jesus Christ. In Him we can take on His virtue of justice.

Freedom is another quality that comes out of justice. Freedom is something sought by all and thought to be gained by some. If freedom is denied, it is considered that a great injustice has been served. Freedom, however:

> *"is dangerous in the hands of those who don't know how to use it (Gal5:13) like a raging fire, freedom without limits is dangerous. 'Freedom doesn't give us the right to do what we please, but to do what pleases God.'"*[130]

Perhaps we are assuming that freedom has no boundaries. Freedom, too often means doing whatever they want and

---

[129] Bill Crowder, "The search for Justice," *Our Daily Bread*, no. June, July, August 2008 (2008).

[130] Joe Stowell, "The Song of the Saints," *Our Daily bread*, no. June, July, August 2009 (2009).

furthermore, no-one can have the right to even tell them otherwise.

Well, we know what happens to those who insist on this definition. Their freedom is taken from them, often by being incarcerated in a prison. True freedom has rules. They dictate that wherever you are, you are completely free as long as you don't cross that line. As kids in school we would draw a line in the dirt and dare the other kid to step over the line. If he did, he lost his freedom of choice and would have to participate in the forthcoming fray. If he exercised his freedom to choose not to cross the line, he was free to go in any other direction he pleased.

Once freedom has been taken, whether it is by imprisonment or some other less dramatic form, distrust can be formed. Like the story I read about regarding a place called 'Chimp Eden.'[131]

{ *Parallax: "the apparent displacement of an observed object due to a change in the position of the observer."* }

This is a place where chimpanzees are rescued from captivity by the 'bush-meat' trade. The animals have been kept in confined spaces for long periods of time and upon their rescue, do not trust their saviour who is trying to release them into an area where they can experience freedom. People can be the same, but once they get past the miss-trust and come out of their confinement, *"for reasons difficult to understand, being freed is more exhilarating than being free."*[132] The rules or otherwise stated as the truth, are for those chimps is that they are free as long as they stay within the much larger confines of Chimp Eden. The Bible says, *"And you shall know the truth, and the*

---

[131] Julie Ackerman Link, "Chimp eden," *Our Daily Bread*, no. June, July, August 2009 (2009).
[132] Julie Ackerman Link, "Celebrate Freedom," *Our daily Bread*, no. June, July, August 2007 (2007).

truth shall make you free. (Joh 8:32)." It is only in the confines of Truth that we can be free.

For those, after reading the above, who are seeking have justice as a virtue in their lives and have found that the more they try, the more oppression they cause, there is only one way to change. To put it plainly; without God, there is no justice.

> *"If all that we have is this world and what we can get and gain here, then we'll do whatever we can to advance and empower ourselves, even if it is at the expense of others."*[133]

Nobody wants to be an oppressor. There is an instinct placed within by God for justice.

> *"We instinctively long for justice but cannot seem to find it. (If we look to imperfect people to get it) The search for justice can be satisfied only by trusting the God who is always just."*[134]

With the parallax of a 'God point of view', we are assured that justice will be served. Nobody gets away with anything and everyone will get the reward they deserve according to the standard laid out in the Bible.

> *"When we spend time with God and see things from His point of view, it changes our perspective completely. We may be jealous of the nonbelievers now, but we won't be at judgement time..."*[135]

We will all be recipients of justice on that day of judgement. Most of us will receive justice while still here in this temporal life. The question is not 'will justice be served?' but rather 'what will justice look like for me?' If you have spent your life

---

[133] Stowell, *Eternity: Reclaiming a passion for what endures*.
[134] Crowder, "The search for Justice."
[135] Joe Stowell, "When Life seems Unfair," *Our daily Bread*, no. March, April, May 2011 (2011).

rejecting God, you won't like the sentence given out to you. After all, when we consider what Jesus has done for us, it is clear that He is the only qualified judge and will decide on what is fair. Gustafson said,

> *"Though sin seems to triumph and wrong conquer right, though lies can put justice to flight, God's truth is eternal, His word shows His might, and He will bring justice to light."*

In reaching the end of this chapter, here is one final quote:

> *"...but Scripture promises that God will one day avenge all injustices (Rom.12:19). While we wait, we are to do what we can to work for justice and leave the results in God's hands."* [136]

---

[136] Link, "Poetic Justice."

Self Control-P-Sensualism

The parallax of self-control is sensualism. The opposite of self-control is other-controlled. The parallax of sensualism is self-control. The opposite of sensualism temperance, moderation, sobriety, soberness

Character	P-Virtue	P-Value	Consequences
• Discerning and disciplined • Determined • Peaceful, safe.	Self Control	Sensualism	• Vulnerable to impulse/addiction • Irresolute • Victimised by results of sin.

Self-control is sought by all or at least recognized as something good to have. In fact some of those whom I have known claim to have control of everything, including them-selves, seem to be totally blind to the obvious, that they are utterly and completely out of control. They are in a position of sensuality, vulnerable to impulsive behaviour and addiction. They are irresolute and made victims. There is a hint of what goes wrong in 1Cor.8:2 *"And if any man thinks that he knows anything, he knows nothing yet as he ought to know."*

There is no denying that people know how to control themselves. It is not in the knowing about it, or knowing about everything else, but rather in how 'he ought to know'. It is about what is done and how it's done, about what is known.

Discerning

It is all too easy to listen to impulse, which is in the domain of sensualism. To discern a thing or to read the situation with accuracy and reliability requires self-control because the volume of impulse can be turned up loud. Once our powers of discernment increase and mature (this is a key word), we are then able to rely to some greater degree on impulse. Impulse, without discernment is dangerous. In the absence of maturity, impulse should be avoided. That, however is easier said then done.

When we are making decisions, self-control is vital. It literally translates into a confidence in the decision made and the ability to act on those decisions. To make decisions based on impulse leaves one vulnerable to second guess their decision, causing temporary or permanent paralysis on acting on that decision.

The ability to discern requires enough self-control to listen. *"...the cost of listening is not nearly as great as the cost of jumping to wrong conclusions."*[137]

We may find that we have actually discerned our top priorities, but then find ourselves distracted by all of life's good options. This is because, instead of developing a virtue, we have developed a value, in which sensualism lives. It takes ongoing self-control to maintain the commitment to your top priorities. I am describing what it takes to put into operation the concept of 'delayed gratification'.

Anne Cetas writes:

> *"We pour our lives into hobbies, pleasures, activities, work – many good things (sensual)... when it seems our life is getting out of balance, the question, 'has that hobby or activity or thing ever loved me back?' may help keep us in check."*[138]

Disciplined

I believe that one of the laws of life is if you don't use self-discipline, others will soon take that role and become the one to discipline you. The issue now is who will discipline you. It

---

[137] Mart de Haun, "Urge to Jump," *Our daily Bread* March April May(2008).
[138] Anne Cetas, "Fever Pitch," *Our daily Bread* December January February(2009).

might be a parent or employer, or even a friend. Personally, if I am going to be disciplined, I would rather it be from someone who genuinely loves me and willing do anything to correct my errors and weaknesses, and that would be God. Take Him out of the Personal Development program and the door is open for whoever wants to do the disciplining, and they may do it out of an incorrect motive and inappropriate means.

A daily discipline formed into a habit requires ongoing effort.

> *"Do you not know that those running in a race all run, but one receives the prize? So run, that you may obtain."* (1Co 9:24) *"...as a consistent habit of life, regular discipline is of far greater value to any athlete than last-minute preparation...the key to going the distance is the discipline of running every day."*[139]

Discipline commences when we are too young to utilize self-discipline. It's called raising children. The lack of starting out discipline leads to one place – sensualism. *"...discipline must begin before character is permanently bent and twisted."*[140] There is a Bible example of this by the way Eli raised his sons. Eli was a priest who failed to discipline his boys resulting in a 'permanent bent and twisted' character, and notice what Jehovah desires from all this.

> *"No, my sons, for it is no good report that I hear. You make Jehovah's people to transgress. If one man sins against another, the judge shall judge him. But if a man sins against Jehovah, who shall plead for him? But they did not listen to the voice of their father, because Jehovah desired to kill them."* (1Sa 2:24-25)

---

[139] David McCasland, "Running every day," *Our daily Bread* June July August(2009).
[140] Julie Ackerman Link, "Failure to discipline," *Our daily Bread*, no. June July August (2011).

Discipline is such an important virtue that it not only affects our own lives, but it is generationally passed along. *"Many important things in life are 'next generation' matters."*[141] The disciplines I insist on will be picked up and carried by the next generation.

When God comes to discipline it is most important not to resist Him. It may, no, it will hurt, but resistance will only bring more and escalating pain.

> *"Now chastening for the present does not seem to be joyous, but grievous. Nevertheless afterward it yields the peaceable fruit of righteousness to those who are exercised by it."* (Heb 12:11)

God, in His Word, even reveals to us, though rarely mentioned anywhere else, how He disciplines his children (Leviticus 26:14-26). This has been called the Five Cycles of Discipline by R. B. Thieme, Jr, and from my own observations seen it in operation.

Parallax: "the apparent displacement of an observed object due to a change in the position of the observer."

"Five cycles of discipline

1. Loss of health, decline of agricultural prosperity, terror, fear, and death in combat, loss of personal freedoms due to negative volition toward Bible doctrine. (Lev26:14-17)
2. Economic recession and depression, increased personal and individual discipline for continued negative volition in spite of first warning. (Lev.26:18-20)
3. Violence and breakdown of law and order, severe restriction of travel and commerce. (Lev.26:21-22)

---

[141] David McCasland, "The next generation," *Our daily Bread*, no. March April May (2008).

4. Military conquest and/or foreign occupation, scarcity of food (reduced to one-tenth the normal supply), separation of families (Lev.26:23-26)
5. Destruction of the nation due to maximum rejection of biblical principles (Lev26:27-39)" [142]

The text is speaking to Gods people as a nation, but the same cycles, I believe, apply to the individual believer.

The first cycle that can be experienced by the believer, means that should the believer fall into carnality, a state of 'being out of fellowship' with God because of unacknowledged sin in your life, part of which is develop a negative attitude toward the Word of God, they will start to lose their health, lack the ability to be prosperous, be filled with fear and lose divine protection as well as loss of personal freedoms.

Cycle two comes into play when the first warning is not enough to turn the believer back. Say hello to poverty. Jobs may be lost. A state of recession and depression is not a pleasant place to live. At this stage it is your own personal 'recession you had to have.'

The third cycle gets worse. Violence and lawlessness enters your life. It could come as the destruction of your home or the theft of your goods. It could also come into your life by way of finding you environment is now full of violence and you always come out worst.

Cycle four is really getting serious. Your starving family is pulled apart and other authorities come in and take over your life. The clearest example is serving time in prison.

The fifth and last cycle is the point of no return. You die. If the believer is having trouble with this idea of God inflicting

---

[142] Jr. R. B. Thieme, *Freedom through Military Victory* (Texas: R. B. Thieme, JR, 2003).

discipline, see **Appendix A** for a full doctrinal statement on the five cycles of discipline.

This may seem rather harsh, but it is only so because we have become so liberal and compromising on what is the most important to God. We have set up our own rules, but we don't have the right to do so. God created the universe and set certain laws and principles in place so that it would all work. Whether we change the rules or not, it makes no difference to what God has set up. He is the God of Grace despite the strictness of His discipline. I know this because He has also set up a way of getting off the cycles.

There is but one way to get off these cycles of discipline and that is to 'Rebound' (another term coined by Thieme) which basically means to apply 1John 1:9. *"If we confess our sins, He is faithful and just to forgive us our sins, and to cleanse us from all unrighteousness."*

Judging by the increasing severity of the five cycles, it would be prudent to examine the way to get off those cycles should you find yourself there?

Here is an expanded translation of 1 John 1:9. 'If we *believers* confess, *that is to say acknowledge and take responsibility for our known* sins *and where we know we have fallen short of God's standard for us*, He is faithful and *completely trustworthy and true to His Word and* just (His justice) to forgive us, *blotting out and forgetting,* our *conscious* sins, and *furthermore*, to cleanse us from all *(conscious or unconscious)* unrighteousness.'

There is no time gap between when you confess and when you are forgiven, for everything has been forgiven beforehand. The forgiveness happened in a space of time about 2000 years ago. To take advantage of that forgiveness requires the need to confess. You will immediately cancel the cycle of discipline and be restored to full relationship with God. There may be some scars left over, but you would rather have those as reminders to never again resist God's plan for your life again. As God's answer to the Apostle Paul regarding his thorn in the side,

> *"And He said to me, My grace is sufficient for you, for My power is made perfect in weakness. Most gladly therefore I will rather glory in my weaknesses, that the power of Christ may overshadow me."* (2Co 12:9)

This knowledge about the cycles of discipline and rebound are vital to take stock of how our lives are going at any point.

> *"Are you feeling a bit panicky about events in your life? Maybe it seems as if you are surrounded by the open waters of relationship problems, or money woes, or simply an inability to put your life in order."*[143]

Which cycle does that look like?

I recently got a good dose of the flu. Does that mean I have sinned and am now in Cycle one? If I am, that is between me and my God, and us only. What I do know is I need to apply rebound daily. If that has been done with all sincerity and I still have the flu, it means I still have the flu and should take my medication, but there is no notion of guilt to go with it.

> *Parallax: "the apparent displacement of an observed object due to a change in the position of the observer."*

Vulnerability to impulsiveness and addiction is the parallax to discernment and discipline. People resist flexibility because it makes them feel vulnerable, yet we all understand that if we are inflexible we will break like a dry dead tree in a windstorm. Flexibility without security in God's plan for us can only lead to

---

[143] Dave Branon, "A place to stand," *Our daily Bread* June July August(2008).

vulnerability. For the believer, he knows *"A man's heart plans his way, but Jehovah directs his steps."* (Pro 16:9)

People can feel vulnerable whenever they have to wait. There is a sense that it is safer to be a moving target. For the believer, waiting has a different result. *"but those who wait on Jehovah shall renew their strength; they shall mount up with wings as eagles; they shall run, and not be weary; they shall walk and not faint."* (Isa 40:31)

Have you ever had that dream where you are falling from a great height but wake up in a cold sweat and heavy breathing, just before you crash to your certain death on the ground? That sense of falling is one way to describe vulnerability. For the believer, it means something very different.

> *"The eternal God is your refuge, and underneath are the everlasting arms. And He shall throw the enemy out from before you, and shall say, Destroy!* (Deu 33:27)

A person that is vulnerable becomes susceptible to impulsive behaviour and addictive personality traits. Impulsiveness and addiction is the crowning glory of sensuality. Discernment and discipline are the result of the virtue of self-control.

Determined

A strong determination results as a by-product of developing the virtue of self-control. To develop the value of sensualism you become irresolute. The line drawn between a virtue and a value can be almost invisible. This is illustrated by the following quote:

> *"Nechayev, a 19th-century disciple of Karl Marx who had a role in the assassination of Czar Alexander II, wrote: 'The revolutionary man...has no personal interests, no business affairs, no emotions, no attachments, no property, and no name. Everything in him is wholly absorbed in the single thought and the*

single passion for revolution.' Although his motives and goals were wrong, Nechayev's statement shows the single-mindedness of commitment."[144]

There is what looks like an incredible level of determination, but I don't know anyone who would put Karl Marx in the same sentence as being a man full of virtue. Yes, I am aware that I just did it and I promise not to do it again. What we really see is a man full of sensuality. 'Passion' is a word that comes under sensuality, and according to his own disciple, that is all he had.

Value fuelled by passion is an unstable bomb, ready to go off with the slightest vibration.

For the determined *"it's always too soon to quit."*[145] This often requires perseverance. Perseverance builds strength into determination.

The parallax of determination is irresolution. To be irresolute means you can't make decisions. That definition covers the full range from inability to make a decision to not being able to stick to a decision. Irresolution is the fruit of sensuality. *"...the implications of our choices are hard to anticipate."*[146] Any decision, if made at all, has no strength. Have you ever asked why we call them 'new year's resolutions' instead of 'new year's goals'? It might be because the word resolution is softer than goal. A goal has great reward when achieved, even more so when it has taken self-control to achieve it. A goal also has equally great penalties if not achieved. A resolution has the rewards too, but it is meaningless because there are no consequences for breaking them.

---

[144] Marvin Williams, "One passion," *Our daily Bread* June July August(2009).
[145] Bill Crowder, "Too soon to quit," *Our daily Bread* June July August(2007).
[146] Bill Crowder, "Looking ahead," *Our daily Bread* June July August(2011).

Safety

The person who develops the value of sensuality will finish up being victimised by life. The person that develops the virtue of self-control will have safety and security in a world that attempts to victimise them. *"You will keep him in perfect peace, whose mind is stayed on You; because he trusts in You."* (Isa 26:3) To 'keep your mind stayed on' anything takes concentration and self-control. Deeper than that, to stay on the virtue side of the table, it is important who you stay your mind on. He must be virtuous, and there is only One who is. Stay your mind on anyone or anything else and the best you will get is everything on the value side.

Knowledge

Paraphrase/Translation

"3 For as you know Him better, He will give you, through His great power, everything you need for living a truly good life: He even shares His own glory and His own goodness with us! 4 And by that same mighty power He has given us all the other rich and wonderful blessings he promised; for instance, the promise to save us from the lust and rottenness all around us, and to give us His own character. 5 But to obtain these gifts, you need more than faith; you must also work hard to be good, and even that is not enough. **For then you must learn to know God better** *and discover what He wants you to do." (2 Pt.1:3-5)*[147]

"...and in [exercising] virtue **[develop] knowledge** *[intelligence]."*[148]

Knowledge – (γνῶσις, gnōsis, *gno'-sis*) Knowing (the act), that is, (by implication) *knowledge:* - knowledge, science.

Facts or experience known by a person, state of knowing, specific information on a subject.

THE 2 PETER 1 LIST CAN BE SEEN AS BELIEVER'S Personal Development Program. It contains

"...all things that pertain unto life and godliness: that is, whatever is needful for the production, preservation and perfecting of spirituality in the souls of God's elect."[149]

It is worth reminding the reader that this program is for believers only. A non-believer cannot even start, because the first requirement is to embrace the faith and be born again. To

---

[147] Publishers, *Living Letters*: 309.
[148] House, *The Amplified bible*.
[149] Arthur W Pink, *Practical Christianity*, sixth, 1990 ed. (Grand Rapids, Michigan: Baker Book House, 1974). 70.

be born again or saved is to become a partaker of the Divine Nature, an essential requirement for progressing to the next stage. This is the parallax. A change in position of the observer must take place in order to even see the Truth. The parallax must be genuine and once the parallax has taken place, it must continue to take place.

The cost of not continuing in the knowledge of God is far greater than for the one who never even started. Later in second Peter we read:

> *"For if they have escaped the pollutions of the world through the full knowledge of the Lord and Saviour Jesus Christ, and are again entangled, they have been overcome by these, their last things are worse than the first. For it would have been better for them not to have fully known the way of righteousness, than fully knowing it, to turn from the holy commandment delivered to them. But the word of the true proverb has happened to them: The dog turning to his own vomit; and, The washed sow to wallowing in the mire."* (2Pe 2:20-22)

> *"Herein lies the radical difference between those described in 2 Peter 1:3,4, and the ones in 2 Peter 2:20 – nothing is said of the latter being 'partakers of the Divine nature!' their 'escaping from the pollutions of the world' was merely a temporary reformation from outward defilements and gross sins, as their turning again to the same makes clear (verse 22)."*[150]

We have seen in the previous section on virtues, what happens if faith is ignored. It isn't virtue any more, and often leads to many undesirable consequences. At best, any change for the better for the one who uses any Personal Development Program that excludes God is 'merely a temporary reformation from outward defilements…'

---

[150] Ibid., 72.

So, first, there is faith, the salvation. Second there is virtue, which might be described as the energy force or 'might' of the Believers Personal Development Program. It is the 'modus operandi' of the Christian. Now let us turn to the next stage – Knowledge.

We have at our disposal, unlike any other time, access to all the knowledge we can handle. Apart from books, schools, universities, and libraries, we have the internet. We may think that the source to all this seemingly infinite amounts of knowledge progressively comes from the continuously developing thinking of geniuses, but it has always been there. Mankind is not the source of all knowledge. I will go further: mankind is not the source of any knowledge, a friendly way of saying man is stupid. God is the source of all knowledge. He is the one and One, the omniscient God. He is not only the source of all knowledge, He knows it too. Further, He promises to release this knowledge to believers. *"For the Lord Jehovah will do nothing unless He reveals His secret to His servants the prophets."* (Amo 3:7)

Basically, omniscient means 'knows everything'. This definition doesn't really cover it when it comes to describing God. Not only does God know everything, He knows everything from eternity past to eternity future, and He knows it because He is the source of all knowledge.

When we are faced with this stage of our development, the development of knowledge, our first approach is often to buy a book and read it or go back to school, or undertake some form of study. These are all fine and things of good merit to do, but you will have missed the point. It is not specifically knowledge that is sought. It is 'to know God better'. To know God better is to develop knowledge from the source. This is the key that opens the door to the cosmic library containing therein all knowledge.

I don't discount the value of gaining knowledge from books, education or study. Personally, I read no less than twenty books every year all of which are for the development of myself in some way. I also study constantly to become more educated. A great deal of knowledge can be gained and it is often heard, 'I know what I am doing', or 'I know what I am talking about.' I try not to have these phrases in my vocabulary because, the more knowledge I gain, the more I realize how little I really know. And then, I find only a small portion of what I have learnt actually sticks and is applicable.

Paul wrote to the Corinthian church, *"And if any man thinks that he knows anything, he knows nothing yet as he ought to know."* (1Co 8:2). On reflection, the knowledge that sticks and is applicable is the knowledge gained from the 'ought to know'. The 'ought to know' is the knowing God better.

> *Parallax: "the apparent displacement of an observed object due to a change in the position of the observer."*

Knowing God is a course with no end in this life.

> *"For now we see in a mirror dimly, but then face to face. Now I know in part, but then I shall fully know even as I also am fully known."* (1Co 13:12).

We may pride ourselves in being knowledgeable, but it is like looking in a dim mirror. We can only ever 'know in part'.

The point is, to develop knowledge without knowing God is a superfluous activity. To get to know God better is the only way to develop the kind of knowledge that will cause personal growth and development.

To 'know God better' is like commencing a mountain climb where you have the foreknowledge that you will not reach the peak in this lifetime, yet we put one foot in front of the other and start climbing. So here is the starting point:

> *"All Scripture is God-breathed, and is profitable for doctrine, for reproof, for correction, for instruction in righteousness, that the man of God may be perfected, thoroughly furnished to every good work."* (2Ti 3:16-17)

We start with the Bible. It is the Bible that makes the 'man of God may be perfect.' Isn't that the pinnacle of Personal Development – to be perfect! God is perfect and getting to know Him through His Word results in some of that perfection rubbing off on us. We have all heard that 'birds of the feather flock together.' We have also heard that we become like those we surround ourselves with. So, surround yourself with God and His Word.

This, of course involves much more than just simply reading the Bible. It must be studied with the attitude that no detail is meaningless or to be missed. Study doctrine, use daily devotionals and commentaries. Keep a journal of what you are learning about God. Attend Bible study groups and prayer meetings. Find a good Bible teacher and glean all you can from them. Find books about what you are learning and go into more depth.

> *" But to obtain these gifts, you need more than faith; you must also work hard to be good, and even that is not enough.* **For then you must learn to know God better** *and discover what He wants you to do."* (2 Pt.1:5)

> *"...as also in all his letters, speaking in them of these things; in which are some things hard to be understood, which the unlearned and unstable pervert, as also they do the rest of the Scriptures, to their own destruction). Therefore, beloved, knowing beforehand, beware lest being led away with the error of the lawless, you fall from your own steadfastness."* (2Pe 3:16-17)

This knowledge is indeed a special kind of knowledge. It is a knowledge that comes from the One who has the highest of character: Jehovah.

Self-Control

Paraphrase/Translation

*"6 Next, **learn to put aside your own desires** so that you will become patient and godly, gladly letting God have His way."*[151]

"and in [exercising] knowledge [develop] self-control,..."[152]

Self-control – (ἐγκράτεια, egkrateia, *eng-krat'-i-ah*) *self control* (especially *continence*): - temperance.

Ability to control ones emotions and reactions

THE BELIEVERS PERSONAL DEVELOPMENT PROGRAM is one that builds line upon line and precept upon precept. There is an order and a sequence to this program and at the same time mastery in one precept is not required before development of the next. First in our sequence is faith. This is saving faith: Followed by virtue, or Christian modus operandi. The gaining of virtue before faith is impossible. Faith must come first. After virtue, as well as alongside it, comes knowledge. Any knowledge gained before virtue becomes dangerous, not too unlike giving power to a corrupt leader. In the television show 'Get Smart', Agent 86 of Control, Maxwell Smart often says, 'if only he had used it for good, instead of evil.'

The virtuous motivation must be firmly in place before the knowledge of God can be exercised for its intended purpose. To convert this knowledge into effective application in our lives, the precept of self-control needs to be developed. To apply knowledge without the faith and virtue is to apply unbridled behaviour and careless thinking. All the knowledge gets

---

[151] Publishers, *Living Letters*: 308.II Peter 1:6
[152] House, *The Amplified bible*.

jumbled up and unintentional behaviour follows. Here is why intelligent people do stupid things. The mind contains an abundance of information, but it only serves to confuse because there is no structure, system or controls in ordering the thoughts. Here is why a perfectly sane person can become confused as soon as there is a minor interruption in their plans. *"Without salvation no sonship; without sonship, no discipleship!"*[153] Without discipleship, no discipline; without discipline, no effective application of knowledge; without knowledge, it's a no-brainer!

All the knowledge gained requires self-control and discipline to effectively apply it. Self-control encapsulates words like temperance and discipline, and a phrase such as 'denial of self.'

> *"This discipline is difficult for the natural heart of each one, for we will not humble ourselves to admit our sin and shame; but it is easy for the honest and good heart that sees itself in the light of Calvary's Sacrifice for sin."*[154]

The best places to develop discipline is in everyday occurrences. Edman's book 'The Disciplines of Life' lists 30 such occurrences where discipline can be developed. Amongst those occurrences is when danger presents itself, when having to make a decision, when a delay of some sort eventuates, when there is strong desire, or desperation. Opportunity for discipline is there when dealing with detail, being determined, in difficulty, in disappointment, when disease visits, when in doubt and in the performance of duty. Further opportunity for discipline exists when applied to knowledge about any or each of these occasions which will not only see you through the occasion, but cause a growth and strength of character to

---

[153] Ph.D. V. Raymond Edman, LL.D, *The Disciplines of Life* (Illinois: Scripture Press, 1948; repr., eight).
[154] Ibid., 10.

develop. Discipline develops the strength of character required to grow.

It seems we live in an ever increasingly un-disciplined society. How *"We need the rugged strength of Christian character that can come only from discipline; the discipline of spirit, of mind, of body..."*[155] to lead the way to a happy full life.

Another word for self-control is temperance. The temperate person is a self-disciplined person. This is a person who has an orderly inner life. They can concentrate. They have a strong sense of responsibility. They are often quiet. They are often misunderstood and thought to be without ambition. Here is another parallax. The Bible says,

> *"And that ye study to be quiet, and to do your own business, and to work with your own hands, as we commanded you; That ye may walk honestly toward them that are without, and that ye may have lack of nothing." (1Th 4:11-12)*

The world's definition of an ambitious person is often quite different than the Bibles definition.

> *"It is the most desirable thing to have a calm and quiet temper, and to be of a peaceable and quiet behaviour. This tends much to our own and others' happiness; and Christians should study how to be quiet. We should be ambitious and industrious how to be calm and quiet in our minds, in patience to possess our own souls, and to be quiet towards others; or of a meek and mild, a gentle and peaceable disposition, not given to strife, contention, or division."*[156]

---

[155] Ibid.Preface
[156] Matthew Henry, *Matthew Henry's Commentary on the whole Bible* (London: Marshall Morgan & Scott, 1960).

To quiet ourselves takes an enormous amount of confidence in knowing what you are doing. Knowing what you are doing takes study and practice. The reason most of us will commit to a course of study is because we have an ambition to achieve something. All this takes self-control.

Unbridled ambition, will not result in 'that ye may lack of nothing', but rather a disturbed mind.

> *"Those who are busy-bodies, meddling in other men's matters, generally have but little quiet in their own minds and cause great disturbances among their neighbours;"* [157]

Every believer has this 'added' or supplied to them.

---

[157] Ibid.

Patience

Paraphrase/Translation

> "6 Next, learn to put aside your own desires so that you will **become patient** and godly, gladly letting God have His way."[158]

> "and in [exercising] knowledge [develop] self-control, and in[exercising] self-control **[develop] steadfastness (patience, endurance), and...**"[159]

Patience – (ὑπομονή, hupomonē, *hoop-om-on-ay'*) Cheerful (or hopeful) *endurance, constancy:* - enduring, patience, patient continuance (waiting).

> Patient: Enduring difficulties or delays calmly. Patience: the quality of being patient.

I JUST HAVE TO GET IN MY CAR, on any morning, and within five minutes of driving, find someone who is driving in a manner dangerous to everyone else on the road. They over-take when there is no room to do so; they race the amber light, and sit two inches from your rear bumper bar and flash their lights at you so you will change lanes, when the other lane is full of cars. They utilize their horns if it takes more than a second to move from the traffic lights (instantly for those who have driven in Melbourne). Really, what is their problem? They lack, amongst other things, patience. They lack patience because they lack self-control. They lack self-control because they lack knowledge. They lack knowledge because they lack virtue. They lack virtue because they lack faith. If they do have a faith, and lack everything else, this would indicate a total lack of development and maturity.

Speaking of maturity, when I was in my first year of my motor mechanics apprenticeship, I was sent to the tools and parts

---

[158] Publishers, *Living Letters*: 308.II Peter 1:6
[159] House, *The Amplified bible*.

office to get a long weight. When I 'got it', both the wait and the joke, I started to develop patience. It was patience for when I would be a third year apprentice and be able to send some unsuspecting first year to the same office for a left-handed screw-driver, chequered paint, a sky hook, or if I wanted to get rid of them, a long weight.

Patience includes wonderful qualities like endurance and steadfastness. The qualities may sound great, but the means of obtaining them can be almost unbearable.

In the face of 'unfathomable losses' due to the tsunami on the 11th of March 2011,

> *"The Japanese people gained a newfound sense of unity and solidarity as they witnessed the patience, courtesy and fortitude of those who lost homes, and loved ones."*[160]

Such qualities came to the surface as Emperor Akihito addressed the nation on the 16th of March. The speech had the same impact on the Japanese as the Emperors message on the 15th of August 1945 where it was acknowledged they were *"enduring the unendurable and suffering the unsufferable"*[161]

This, by the way, and though most Japanese would not know it or admit that this is the Bibles way of becoming patient. *"And not only this, but we glory in afflictions also, knowing that **afflictions work out patience**,"* (Rom 5:3)

Should we turn the gaining of patience into a formula, it would look like this:

(Self-control +Persistence) X Patience = Perseverance

---

[160] Yoichi Funahashi, "March 11 - Japan's Zero Hour," *Time*, July 8 2011 2011.
[161] Ibid.

It is the one with the character trait of perseverance that is the highest developed, and more often than not, the one who takes the prize home.

Another area of patience to consider is in the ability to demonstrate 'delayed gratification.' My mother always told me, and this is how I know it is true, that good things came in small packages and all good things come to those who wait. The Bible has another 'take' on delayed gratification,

> *"And we know that all things work together for good to those who love God, to those who are called according to His purpose."* (Rom 8:28)

All good things don't necessarily work together for good for those who wait, but they do for those who 'love God' and are 'called according to His purpose.'

Here again is the parallax. Patience isn't real patience unless there is a love for God and active part of His purpose or plan. The delayed gratification that comes to the believer is an understatement.

Another way patience can be developed is through a means most people don't like to talk about, especially Christians. That is the development of patience through the application of pressure, at times almost unbearable pressure. Watchman Nee writes:

> *"In sickness he is holy; in health he becomes worldly. The Lord has to keep him in prolonged illness in order to keep him holy. His holiness hinges on his sickness! Let us understand, however, that life with the Lord need not at all be restricted to illness. Never, never entertain the thought that unless one is under the yoke of sickness he has no strength to glorify God in his daily duties. On the contrary, he should be able to manifest the life of God in an ordinary daily walk. To be able to endure*

suffering is good, but is it not even better if one can obey God when he is full of strength?

Be it therefore apprehended that the spiritual blessing we receive in sickness is far inferior to what we receive in restoration. If we rest on God for healing, then naturally after being cured we will continue to walk in holiness so as to preserve our health."[162]

Patience is developed best in my opinion, through what R. B. Thieme Jr., calls the 'Faith-Rest Technique.' The faith-rest technique trains you to stand still, something required by patience. *"There is no work, no movement involved at all – just believing, or trusting the Lord, and then, to keep on trusting and waiting on Him."*[163] This technique is developed in two ways: a] Promises, and b] Doctrine.

Promises: There are over 7000 promises in the Bible and all are useless and powerless until you learn and apply them. The promises that you know are the only promises that are of any use to you. Here we can say, 'what you don't know will hurt and kill you.'

To learn and apply promises, firstly read your Bible and when you find one, record it in a 'promise journal'. Visit this journal regularly and memorise as many promises as you can. Secondly, look for situations in your life where you can apply those promises. By applying it, I mean think about the promise and behave according to that promise as you approach the situation.

Promises will help you, but only so far. There is another step.

Doctrine: Doctrine is the study of God's Word which shows us how to live our lives and how to approach it. Every doctrine has a practical expression. For example, when you understand the

---

[162] Nee, *The Spiritual man*.
[163] R. B. Thieme, *The Faith-Rest Life*: 1.

doctrine of forgiveness, not only do you feel personally free from guilt and shame, but you are also able to forgive others.

When patience is developed by using the faith-rest technique, you have a 'relaxed mental attitude.' You can truly sing, 'don't worry, be happy.'

Patience is the fruit of self-control

Patience is the seed of godliness

Godliness

Paraphrase/Translation

*"6 Next, learn to put aside your own desires so that you will become patient and **godly, gladly letting God have His way.**"*[164]

*"and in [exercising] knowledge [develop] self-control, and in[exercising] self-control [develop] steadfastness (patience, endurance), and in [exercising] steadfastness [develop] **godliness** (piety)."*[165]

Godliness – (εὐσέβεια, eusebeia, *yoo-seb'-i-ah*) *Piety*; specifically the *gospel* scheme: - godliness, holiness.

Pious and devout to God

THE LAST WORDS OF Titus Flavius Vespasian, the Roman Emperor were, *"I think I am becoming a God."*[166] Unfortunately, Titus isn't the only one thinking this way. Many arrive at such deluded conclusions of believing they are becoming a god or already a god, usually as a symptom of madness.

There are also many who interpret the subject of this chapter about 'godliness' as having become or becoming like God. We would expect a few crack-pots to make such claims that do so to promote their 'cult' or to use a friendlier term 'new religious movements', and increase their following. We have also seen the disastrous effects of such people. Remember 'Jones town'? Jim Jones is quoted as saying, *"It is written that ye are gods. I'm a god and you're a god"* (Jim Jones, quoted in J. Reston, Jr.

---

[164] Publishers, *Living Letters*: 308.II Peter 1:6
[165] House, *The Amplified bible*.
[166] James Inglis, *Fighting Talk* (Millers Point: Murdoch Books Australia, 2008). 41.

and N. Adams, "Father Cares: The Last of Jonestown" program on National Public Radio, 23 April, 1981.)

> **Important note before you read on:**
>
> All following quotes referring to you or I being a god are secondary document quotes (see note in the introduction) and have been copied from www.iam-iam-iam.com. This is a web site that supports this belief and has used these quotes from many to provide support for their belief. However, upon checking some of the source documents referred to, I found references to be incorrect. For example, quotes from M Scott Peck are brought to question because the quotes do not appear on the pages referenced. There could be several explanations varying from differences in version or edition of the source document, to relying on the secondary quote of another. Either way, this is a negative reflection on whoever publishes these. I want to make clear that this is not my intention by using these quotes and pointing out these errors. I merely want to make the point that the belief that we are gods is sufficiently significant to highlight. It does not reflect my own opinion, nor as far as I can tell reflect what the Bible has to say. What follows is written 'as if' each of these quote sources is verified.

There are others of note, in some circles, which make similar statements or claims:

"Be still and know that you are God when you know that you are God, YOU WILL BEGIN TO LIVE GODHOOD..."' (Meditations of Maharishi Mahesh yogi p.178)

"Be constantly in the thought of God and you too will become God" (Baba's grace Discourses of Shrii Shrii Ananda Murti)

"May this manifestation lead you to see each other as the gods you are" (Maitreya Message 13 feb. 1982)

"One of these days I'll be so complete I won't be a human. I'll be a god." (John Denver, Newsweek dec.20,1976 p,68)

"Know that you are God" (From Dancing in the Light New ager, Shirley MacLaine)

Other who think they are god

"You are the christ: The only begotten son of your own God-self" (New ager, M.S. Princess, Step By Step We Climb, p.127)

"Eventually . . . all perspectives lead us . . . return to the truth of truths . . . that we are God." (Jon Klimo, Channeling (Jeremy P. Tarcher, 1987), p. 296.)

"the Son of God is each and every human being when he has attained the highest level of surrender to God's will" (Guru Maharaj Ji)

"God and man are one. Man is incarnate God." (Sung Myung Moon of the Moonies, Christianity in Crises p.5)

Even more who think they are god

"we may know we are gods... We are all gods. Because we are all gods, we cannot know that we were gods. That's why I respect all the people and like them a lot and like them because they are all gods." (Supreme master Ching Hai)

"Who is God? You! You!" (Supreme master Ching Hai)

"you are gods, in this earth, and it's about time we start operating like gods instead of a bunch of mere powerless humans" (Creflo Dollar, Changing your world April 17, 2002 LeSea Broadcasting)

"Look behind you, your neighbour in front, to your right and left, that is what God looks like. Alright, you are satisfied? God said, 'God made man in His own image.' So if you want to find God, look at your neighbours. Each one of us houses God inside." (Supreme master Ching Hai)

"We are gods!" (Barbara Marx Hubbard, The Revelation: A Message of Hope for the New Millennium, Nataraj Publishing, Novato, CA, 1995, p. 312

"We are all Gods" (Alice A. Bailey, The Reappearance of the Christ, Lucis Publishing Company, New York, 1948; p. 9)

"All men are spiritually evolving until . . .each will fully express his divinity . . ." (Ernest Holmes What Religious Science Teaches p.21)

"In each of us is the potentiality to become a God .... Man can transform himself... he has in him the seeds of Godhood that can grow" (Mormon President Spencer W. Kimball Salt Lake City Tribune, September 18,1974)

"the Spirit of God dwells in me, as me. I and the Father are one, and all that the Father has is mine. In truth, I am the Christ of God" (The Planetary Commission, p. 157 John Price the World Healing Meditation)

"The Lord created you and me for the purpose of becoming Gods like himself " (Mormonism, Journal of Discourses, vol.3, p.93)

"God and man are of the same race, differing only in their degree of advancement" (Mormon Apostle, Dr. John Widtsoe Gospel Through the Ages, pg.107).

"Trust God. Or if you wish, trust yourself, for Thou Art God." (Neale Donald Walsch, Conversations with God: An Uncommon Dialogue, Book 3, Hampton Roads Publishing Company, Inc., 1998; p. 350)

"You are already a God. You simply do not know it." (Neale Donald Walsch, Conversations with God: an uncommon dialogue, Book 3 1996, p.202.)

"Today I lay claim to all the attributes of God . . . [and] as a Divine being . . . I rejoice in my Divine nature" (Charles Fillmore Science of Mind, December 1986)

"Thus, you are part of God ... YOU ARE GOD. Every living and discarnate individual is God. Together we are an energy gestalt called God...." (Dick Sutphen Self Help update Jan.1985 p.6-9)

"I AM THAT I AM, and there is no other besides me" (Charles Fillmore, Unity school of Christianity, Christian Healing)

"Think, speak, and act as the God You Are" (Neale Donald Walsch, Conversations with God)

"I believe happiness can be achieved through concentration upon oneself, opening to others elevating oneself to God." (Robert Muller, New Genesis p.180)

"We are gods of course, but gods of our own universe, and gods among other gods. Every man, woman and child is God!" (Paul Twitchell, The Flute of God, Minneapolis: ECKANKAR, 1969, p. 7)

If these are unpalatable statements for believers, what follows will have you screaming 'blasphemy!' (Just don't get sidetracked from the point).

That is a warning that the following collection of quotes will be disturbing to say the least, but even more disturbing is who said them. One of the main points of this book is to say that Personal Development without God is devoid of real power. In many ways, I give the unbeliever a bit of a hard time on this point. This chapter however, is different, because I launch an untethered attack on the sayings of some so called popular and prominent 'Christians.' I do so without apology because these people have no excuse for the gross misinterpretation or plain outright ignorance of Scripture. What follows is so far from the Truth, that it may even cause nausea in some. Such was the effect on me, that I stopped research on this after looking at only one source: www.iam-iam-iam.com

I almost excluded this next section, but I felt that it is helpful to understand what 'godliness' is by seeing first what it is not, as well as expose some false teachers. Just as a side note, 2 Peter is in part written to expose false teachers and as it is the main text for this book, doing likewise is unavoidable if I am to stay within the context.

Quotes from 'believers'?

"God wants us to become Himself ... We are growing toward God. God is the goal of evolution" (The Road Less Traveled, 1978. p. 270). M. Scott Peck)

Even more of them

"To know God, to love God, and to understand God is finally to realize one's own godhood." (Rodney R. Romney, pastor of Seattle's First Baptist Church, journey to Inner Space: Finding Godwin-Us (1986), p. 26.)

"Every Christian is a god. ... "You don't have a God in you; you are one," (The Force of Love (Fort Worth: Kenneth Copeland Ministries, 1987, audiotape #02-0028), side 1.)

"when I read in the Bible where He [Jesus] says, 'I AM,' I say, 'Yes, I AM too!'" (Kenneth Copeland: Spoken during a crusade meeting, 19/7/1987)

"There is a god class of beings." (Kenneth Copeland Force of Love; Tape #02-0028), (TBN), recorded 2/5/86)

"you are all-God" (Kenneth Copeland, Now We Are in Christ Jesus (Fort Worth: KCP Publications, 1980), 16-17)

"Dogs beget dogs, and cats beget cats, and God begets gods. You are all little gods" (Kenneth Copeland, speaking on Trinity Broadcasting Network's Praise the Lord show)

"What is it that God wants of us?" "It is for the individual to become totally, wholly God" (M. Scott Peck, The Road Less Traveled p.283)

"The believer is called Christ...That's who we are; we're Christ!" (Kenneth M. Hagin, Zoe: The God-Kind of Life (Tulsa, OK: Kenneth Hagin Ministries, Inc., 1989), 35-36, 41.)

"Man...was created on terms of equality with God, and he could stand in God's presence without any consciousness of inferiority...God has made us as much like Himself as possible...He made us the same class of being that He is Himself!" (Kenneth M. Hagin, Zoe: The God-Kind of Life (Tulsa, OK: Kenneth Hagin Ministries, Inc., 1989), 35-36,

"Man was created in the god class, was not created in the animal class, it was the gods class. ...Alright, are we gods? We are a class of gods."

(Kenneth Copeland Praise the Lord, TBN, 2/5/1986)

"You don't have a god in you, you are one," (Kenneth Copeland, The Force of Love (Fort Worth, TX: Kenneth Copeland Ministries, 1987), audiotape #02-0028, side 1.)

"I am a little messiah walking on earth,..... You are a little god on earth running around" (Benny Hinn Praise-a-Thon TBN, Nov. 6 1990)

"Though we are not Almighty God Himself, nevertheless, we are now divine" (Benny Hinn, TBN, 12/1/90)

"Are you ready for some real revelation knowledge....you are god" (Benny Hinn, "Our Position In Christ", tape # AO31190-1)

"Christians are little messiahs. Christians are little gods." (Benny Hinn Praise-a-thon (TBN),11/90, "Our position in Christ," tape A031190-1)

"Let's say, I am a God man.' ...This spirit man within me is a God-Man. ... I'm a God-Man." (Benny Hinn Praise the Lord, TBN, Dec 6 1990).

"Are you a child of God? Then you're divine! Are you a child of God? Then you're not human!" (Benny Hinn TBN, Dec 1, 1990).

"When you were born again the Word was made flesh in you ... You are everything He was and everything He is and ever He shall be .... Don't say,' I have.' Say, ' I am, I am, I am, I am, I am." (Benny Hinn, "Our Position in Christ #2-The Word Made Flesh" [Orlando, FL: Orlando Christian Center, 1991, audiotape #A031190-2, side 2.)

"God came to earth and touched a piece of dust and turned it into a God." (Benny Hinn TBN, Dec 1, 1990).

None of the above cited speakers and authors can claim originality to their claims. Aspiring to be a god has been around long before man was even created. Lucifer was the first to make such a claim.

> *"How you are fallen from the heavens, O shining star, son of the morning! How you are cut down to the ground, you who weakened the nations!* **For you have said in your heart, I will go up to the heavens, I will exalt my throne above the stars of God; I will also sit on the mount of the congregation, in the sides of the north. I will go up above the heights of the clouds; I will be like the Most High.** *Yet you shall be brought down to hell, to the sides of the Pit."* (Isa 14:12-15)

Created beings can never be god. To be God, you cannot be a created being.

When the Bible speaks of godliness it is not speaking of becoming a god. Most that support this heresy use two verses of scripture to support their argument. Those verses are:

"Jesus answered them, Is it not written in your Law, "I said, You are gods?" (Joh 10:34)

"I have said, You are gods; and all of you sons of the Most High." (Psa 82:6)

The verse in John is a quote of the verse in Psalms. The first thing to notice is the use of lowercase 'g' for gods. This however, only provides a weak argument against those who believe they are gods. They may come back with the Greek and Hebrew words used in these verses, which are:

Greek word for god: Θεός theos *theh'-os*. Of uncertain affinity; a *deity*, especially *the* supreme *Divinity*; figuratively a *magistrate*; by Hebraism *very*: - X exceeding, God, god [-ly, -ward].

Hebrew word for god: אלהים 'ĕlôhîym *el-o-heem'*. Plural... *gods* in the ordinary sense; but specifically used (in the plural thus, especially with the article) of the supreme *God*; occasionally applied by way of deference to *magistrates*; and sometimes as a superlative: - angels, X exceeding, God (gods) (-dess, -ly), X (very) great, judges, X mighty.

This seems a much stronger and intelligent argument for the 'being a god' theory, but it is really too simplistic. The context of Jesus' words has not been examined yet, nor has the source of this came to be written in 'the law'.

The context is the easiest to deal with. Jesus was in the temple speaking with the judges and lawyers of the day, who were trying to trap Him into saying something that would give them reason to get rid of Him. They accuse Jesus of blasphemy because He claims to be the Christ, the Son of God. To them and according to the Law, anyone claiming to be God should be stoned to death.

Jesus quotes Psalms 82:6 and it is here that we see the source of His word choice. Jesus responds by quoting the law:

> *"It is written (Psa_82:6), I have said, You are gods. It is an argument a minore ad majus - from the less to the greater. If they were gods, much more am I."*[167]

Jesus uses this verse in Psalms deliberately because those He was speaking to would instantly know what He meant:

> *"He called them gods to whom the word of God came, and the scripture cannot be broken.* ***The word of God's commission came to them, appointing them to their offices, as judges, and therefore they are called gods****, (Exo.22:28). To some the word of God came immediately, as to Moses; to others in the way of an instituted ordinance. Magistracy is a divine institution; and magistrates are God's delegates, and therefore the scripture calleth them gods;"*[168]

John Wesley's Explanatory Notes say the same thing about Psalms 82:

> *"Standeth - To observe all that is said or done there. Mighty - Kings or chief rulers. By their congregation he understands all persons whatsoever of this high and sacred order. Judgeth - Passes sentence upon them.* ***The gods - Judges and magistrates are called gods, because they have their commission from God, and act as his deputies.****"*[169]

The answer to the correct interpretation of these verses is nowhere near that of those quoted earlier. Kings, rulers, judges and magistrates were called gods because of their role in society. This has nothing to do with divinity.

---

[167] Henry, *Matthew Henry's Commentary on the whole Bible.*
[168] Ibid.
[169] E-Sword Ver. 10.0.5.

Now that we have determined what godliness definitely is not, let's turn to what it is.

Out of patience comes godliness.

Godliness is a way of life: *"for kings and all who are in authority, so that we may lead a quiet and peaceable **life in all godliness** and reverence." (1Ti 2:2)*

Godliness is a great mystery: *"And without controversy **great is the mystery**[170] **of godliness**: God was manifested in the flesh, justified in the Spirit, seen by angels, preached among nations, believed on in the world, and received up into glory." (1Ti 3:16)*

Godliness is practiced: *"But refuse profane and old-womanish tales, and **exercise**[171] **yourself to godliness**." (1Ti 4:7)*

Godliness is valuable: *"For bodily exercise profits a little, but **godliness is profitable** to all things, having promise of the present life, and of that which is to come." (1Ti 4:8)*

Godliness is the right form of doctrine: *"If anyone teaches otherwise, and does not consent to wholesome words (those of our Lord Jesus Christ), and to the **doctrine according to godliness**," (1Ti 6:3)*

Godliness is not the gaining of...: *"meddling, of men whose minds have been corrupted and deprived of the truth, supposing that **gain is godliness. Withdraw from such**." (1Ti 6:5)*

Godliness is great gain: *"But godliness with contentment **is great gain**." (1Ti 6:6)*

---

[170] Mystery: From a derivative of μύω muō (to *shut* the mouth); a *secret* or "mystery" (through the idea of *silence* imposed by *initiation* into religious rites): - mystery.

[171] Exercise: to *practise naked* (in the games), that is, *train* (figuratively): - exercise.

Godliness is followed: *"But you, O man of God, flee these things and **follow after** righteousness, godliness, faith, love, patience, and meekness." (1Ti 6:11)*

Godliness is how we ought to behave: *"Then, all these things being about to be dissolved, **what sort ought you** to be in holy behaviour and godliness," (2Pe 3:11)*

Godliness is behaving and living life in such a way as to communicate to all those that see: you love and serve the One and Only God.

Godliness has form: *"having **a form of godliness**, but denying the power of it; even turn away from these." (2Ti 3:5)*

Godliness has the right Truth: *"Paul, a servant of God and an apostle of Jesus Christ (according to the faith of God's elect, in the acknowledging of **the truth** which is according to godliness." (Tit 1:1)*

Godliness should be professed: *"but with good works, which becomes women **professing**[172] godliness." (1Ti 2:10)*

When godliness is formed into our lives, it is made obvious by and attitude of gladly letting God have His way according to His plan.

The heart is thus in communion with God. Out of godliness comes brotherly kindness.

---

[172] Professing: to *announce upon* (reflexively), that is, (by implication) to *engage* to do something, to *assert* something respecting oneself: - profess, (make) promise.

Brotherly Kindness

Paraphrase/Translation

*"7 This will make possible the next step, which is for you **to enjoy other people and to like them,** and finally you will grow to love them deeply."*[173]

*"7 And in [exercising] godliness [develop] **brotherly affection**.."*[174]

Brotherly kindness – (φιλαδελφία, Philadelphia, *fil-ad-el-fee'-ah). Fraternal affection:* - brotherly love (kindness), love of the brethren.

Brotherhood: Fellowship, association, Kindness: considerate, friendly, and helpful

JOHN DARBY, IN HIS SYNOPSIS of the Old and New Testament, writes about our text in 2 Peter on brotherly kindness,

"The heart being thus in communion with God, affection flows out freely towards those who are dear to Him, and who, sharing the same nature, necessarily draw out the affections of the spiritual heart: brotherly love is developed."[175]

The fruit of godliness is brotherly kindness.

God loves people, so being godly, which comes from communing with God, will produce in us the ability to 'enjoy other people and to like them.' Brotherly kindness then brings us into the place of the subject of the next chapter, love. Therefore, brotherly kindness provides the strong capacity for love. Since God is love, it stands that it is God who teaches us brotherly kindness. *"But regarding brotherly love, you do not*

---

[173] Publishers, *Living Letters*: 310.II Peter 1:7
[174] House, *The Amplified bible*: 1459.II Peter 1:7
[175] E-Sword.

need that I write to you, for you yourselves are taught by God to love one another." (1Th 4:9)

He teaches us brotherly kindness through us exercising godliness. Real brotherly kindness can only be taught by God, excluding all the attempts of others.

One of the objectives of a Personal Development Program is to 'be a person that loves people.' If the program they are on excludes God, their like or love of people will be shallow, lacking real depth, and often manipulative in nature. At best, this human response to others will be short-term and easily swayed. It has to be this way because brotherly kindness is taught by God and any attempt by a lesser being to pass it on, will result in a lesser quality and quantity. Kindness without God is human kindness.

[*Parallax: "the apparent displacement of an observed object due to a change in the position of the observer."*]

"Human kindness is like a defective tap, the first gush may be impressive but the stream soon dries up." (P. D. James)

Human kindness has limits and is conditional. *"As a result of half a century of Soviet rule people have been weaned from a belief in human kindness."* (Svetlana Alliluyeva)

Philip Francis said it well, *"I go now before the milk of Human kindness goes sour for me."* (Philip Francis)[176]

The word 'brotherly' identifies the object of our kindness. Brotherly refers to a fellow believer, but not to the exclusion of the non-believer. For the purpose of our discussion in the area of Personal Development, godliness will produce the capacity to be kind to our fellow believers. It is a starting point. If you can't be kind to a brother, don't expect to be able to show kindness to someone who is not a brother.

---

[176] Source of three previous quotes: www.brainyquotes.com

Many have tried to be kind to everyone they come in contact with only to be disappointed in the response or left vulnerable to being hurt. There is a certain amount of risk in showing kindness and this is precisely why the development of this grace should be conducted in a safe environment. The group of believers should be the safest environment for this.

There are a few issues to consider when being kind doesn't work out; a] the motive of your kindness, b] Your definition of kindness, and c] the object of your kindness.

The motive of your kindness: If you have a motive for kindness, it's not the type of kindness God would show us. Og Mandino and Princess Diana came close to motiveless kindness.

> *"Beginning today, treat everyone you meet as if they were going to be dead by midnight. Extend to them all the care, kindness and understanding you can muster, and do it with no thought of any reward. Your life will never be the same again."* (Og Mandino)

> *"Carry out a random act of kindness, with no expectation of reward, safe in the knowledge that one day someone might do the same for you."* (Princess Diana)

Another touching story of showing unconditional kindness is found on www.bible.org.:

> *"Despite his busy schedule during the Civil War, Abraham Lincoln often visited the hospitals to cheer the wounded. On one occasion he saw a young fellow who was near death. "Is there anything I can do for you?" asked the compassionate President. "Please write a letter to my mother," came the reply. Unrecognized by the soldier, the Chief Executive sat down and wrote as the youth told him what to say.*

The letter read, "My Dearest Mother, I was badly hurt while doing my duty, and I won't recover. Don't sorrow too much for me. May God bless you and Father. Kiss Mary and John for me." The young man was too weak to go on, so Lincoln signed the letter for him and then added this postscript: "Written for your son by Abraham Lincoln."

Asking to see the note, the soldier was astonished to discover who had shown him such kindness. "Are you really our President?" he asked. "Yes," was the quiet answer. "Now, is there anything else I can do?" The lad feebly replied, "Will you please hold my hand? I think it would help to see me through to the end." The tall, gaunt man granted his request, offering warm words of encouragement until death stole in with the dawn. (Source unknown)"

The greatest act of unconditional kindness ever shown in history, and will never be repeated was when Jesus Christ took the penalty of all man-kinds sin from the past, present, and future, upon Himself. There, on the cross, He died once and for all.

Your definition of kindness: Is your definition, without looking at the dictionary, being nice? If so, I am afraid you have limited yourself. Sometimes you have to be cruel to be kind. Let's say, for example, there is an addict in your family. Any 'niceness' shown to them may have the result of enabling them to continue in their destructive habit. The answer is often to withhold resources from them, seeming to be cruel, but it is the kindest thing you can do for them. Kindness should never be mistaken for weakness.

The object of your kindness: Your thinking may consist of, 'I must be kind to non-believers because it will be a good witness and they will get saved.' The motive is fine, but the action is when you boil it down, manipulative. There is always a flip side, or a parallax to how kindness is perceived. The abovementioned thinking could also communicate that if being saved was out of the question, you would no longer be obligated to be kind. In fact, you probably have good reason to be just plain nasty.

Kindness, developed from godliness, is more about who you are than what you do or say.

The power of kindness

Kindness, whether divinely developed or human, has power, though the former is far greater and infinite.

Kindness can help others to submit to you and even soften their attitude towards you.

> *"A spirit, breathing the language of independence, is natural to Englishmen, few of whom are disposed to brook compulsion, or submit to the dictates of others, when not softened by reason, or tempered with kindness."* (Joseph Lancaster)

Kindness causes misunderstanding, mistrust, and hostility to melt away.

> *"Constant kindness can accomplish much. As the sun makes ice melt, kindness causes misunderstanding, mistrust, and hostility to evaporate."* (Albert Schweitzer)[177]

There is no doubt. Kindness is a powerful grace to possess, but like all things powerful, it must be used with discipline. The lack of kindness leaves behind many 'I might haves' or 'if only'. *"I might have been improved for my whole life, I might have been made another creature...by a kind word."* (Charles Dickens, David Copperfield)

---

[177] Source for last two quotes: www.brainyquotes.com

About kind words, there cannot be enough. *"A word is dead when it is said, some say. I say it begins to live that day."* (Emily Dickinson)

Brotherly kindness is the seed of love.

Love

Paraphrase/Translation

*"7 This will make possible the next step, which is for you to enjoy other people and to like them, and finally you will **grow to love them deeply.**"*[178]

*"7 And in [exercising] godliness [develop] brotherly affection and in [exercising] brotherly affection [develop] **Christian love**."*[179]

Love – (ἀγάπη, agapē, *ag-ah'-pay*) *Love*, that is, *affection* or *benevolence*; specifically (plural) a *love feast:* - (feast of) charity ([-ably]), dear, love.

> Have great affection for (this definition has 8 meanings ranging from sexual passion to a score of nothing in tennis).

IT IS OFTEN SAID THAT GOD IS LOVE, and indeed this is true, but what is meant by love? When the Bible speaks of love, it not only uses several different words for love, but also means something different to what we might expect. In the previous chapter we looked at 'philadelphia'. In this chapter the word used is 'agape'. To understand what 'agape' is, the first thing according to our text comes after 'brotherly kindness'. It is also noteworthy to see that 'agape' is the last of the chorus of seven. We can take from this that this is the grace that we end up being if we follow this Personal Development Program.

Next, it will be helpful to get some idea of what the Love of God is. His love:

> *"does not fall in love or begin to love. His love does not require inspiration or an object. His love is not*

---
[178] Publishers, *Living Letters*: 310.II Peter 1:7
[179] House, *The Amplified bible*: 1459.II Peter 1:7

disappointed, frustrated, or diminished by knowledge of the sins and failures of His creatures. His love is not complicated by ignorance, silliness, or absurdities. Neither is His love emotional or sentimental."[180]

Already, we can see that His love far exceeds our own definition or expression of love.

God's love is expressed in three categories: Divine self-love, divine impersonal love and divine personal love.[181]

Divine Self-love

God is a triune God. He is God the Father, God the Son, and God the Holy Spirit. This books scope does not include a detailed argument for this belief, so it will stick to the subject and in this case a very important subject within the area of Personal Development. Basically, we can call this category Divine Self-love because each member of the God-head has perfect love for one another. But rather than saying, inadequately, 'divine love for one another', we can say Divine Self-love because of the Trinity. Trinity, in the Bible, though the word itself does not appear there, means

> *"that one God exists as three distinct persons who are coequal, cofinite, and coeternal, all possessing the same essential nature (Ps.110:1; Jn.10:30)."*[182]

Therefore, because each member loves each other and they are one, it is more accurate to say Divine Self-love.

When we consider this for a moment, we see that the Divine Self-love is inclusive and shared only between the members of

---

[180] Jr R. B. Thieme, *The Trinity* (Texas: R. B. Thieme Jr., Bible Ministries, 1972, 1975, 1993, 2003). 9.
[181] Each category title is originated by R. B. Thieme Jr. and outlined in the above citation.
[182] R. B. Thieme, *The Trinity*: 1.

the God-head, and exclusive to all other created beings. So what? You may ask.

This revelation of this category of God's love calls into question the validity of a large field of psychological study and practice, as well as a library full of material on 'self-esteem.'

If self-love is exclusively a Divine love, what business is it of created beings, mainly human beings have in pursuing it? Until I find in the Word of God support for working on my 'self-esteem', I must shun this who field. At this point, as I have not found anything in the Word of God that instructs me to lift my 'self-esteem', but rather the contrary. Job 25:6 says: *"how much less man who is a maggot, and the son of man, who is a worm?"* Psalm 22:6 *"But I am a worm, and no man; a reproach of men, and despised by the people."* So I conclude, for now, that for me to pursue the illusive 'high self-esteem' is to try and do something that belongs solely to the Divine. To try and become a god is beyond absurd. It is blasphemous and one of the dumbest things anyone could do. Lucifer tried it, and look what happened, and continues to happen to him!

The next two categories are inclusive of mankind. When I say inclusive, I mean that man can gain the capacity and express these categories of love.

Divine impersonal love

Divine impersonal love is directed to all of man-kind and is extended unconditionally whether they are a believer or not.

> *"For God so loved the world that He gave His only-begotten Son, that whoever believes in Him should not perish but have everlasting life."* (Joh 3:16)

> *"In this the love of God was revealed in us, because God sent His only begotten Son into the world that we might live through Him."* (1Jn 4:9)

> *"But God commends His love toward us in that while we were yet sinners Christ died for us."* (Rom 5:8)

This is indeed a great love, which can only be gained by personally experiencing it in our lives. This is how God loves the world. This is how believers can become lovers of those in the world. There is a saying that can now be seen as false: 'you must learn to love yourself, before you can love others.' The Truth is 'you must love the Lord Jesus Christ before you can love others.'

Divine personal love

This third category is inclusive, but selectively so. It is conditional. It only includes the believer. It is the love shared between God and His children.

> *"being justified freely by His grace through the redemption that is in Christ Jesus; whom God has set forth to be a propitiation through faith in His blood, to declare His righteousness through the passing by of the sins that had taken place before, in the forbearance of God; for the display of His righteousness at this time, for Him to be just and, forgiving the one being of the faith of Jesus."* (Rom 3:24-26)

> *"For He has made Him who knew no sin, to be sin for us, that we might become the righteousness of God in Him."* (2Co 5:21)

> *"God loves His own perfect righteousness wherever it is found. Therefore, from the moment of salvation every believer is the object of divine personal love forever."*[183]

Once you are a child of God, there is no changing that fact. Even if one is to wonder from His household, this love causes God to pursue relentlessly after this one. If the believer who is

---

[183] Ibid., 11.

running from God is at a loss as to why he has so much trouble, the answer lies here. God is doing whatever it takes to bring you back. The more you resist the more trouble that comes.

I was asked why a backslidden Christian was always getting caught and imprisoned for the crimes committed while the non-believing friends kept getting away with breaking the law with more severity. Here is where we see the divine personal love in action. The back-slider is still a child of God and He is pursuing him to the point of doing whatever it will take to get their attention and put them in a position where they can no longer run, but turn back to Him, so they get caught.

Meanwhile, though God has a divine impersonal love for all, when He has to choose between his own child and a child of the world, He will put His children first. This is not too difficult to understand, for as a father, I would do exactly the same. I would, without hesitation, if placed in the position, save my own children before even considering another's.

This illustrates another great category of love, one that has been fully supplied to the believer to both receive and express. It is the ultimate state of the Bibles Personal Development program.

In order to enter and remain in this ultimate state, there is an all important condition, besides being a believer. This condition requires on-going diligence, careful attention, and immediate action to fulfil.

The believer must remain in a state of relaxed mental attitude. This is achieved by 'rebound' (1Jn.1:9) from 'Mental attitude sins.' These include: *"pride, jealousy, bitterness, hatred, vindictiveness, implacability, envy, guilt feelings, fear, worry, anxiety, self-pity."*[184]

---

[184] Jr R. B. Thieme, *The Plan of God* (Texas: R. B. Thieme Jr., Bible Ministries, 1972, 1973, 1992, 2003). 9.

"If we confess our sins, He is faithful and just to forgive us our sins, and to cleanse us from all unrighteousness." (1Jn 1:9)

Now it is time to plot your position on the chart shown in the chapter on the history of Personal Development.

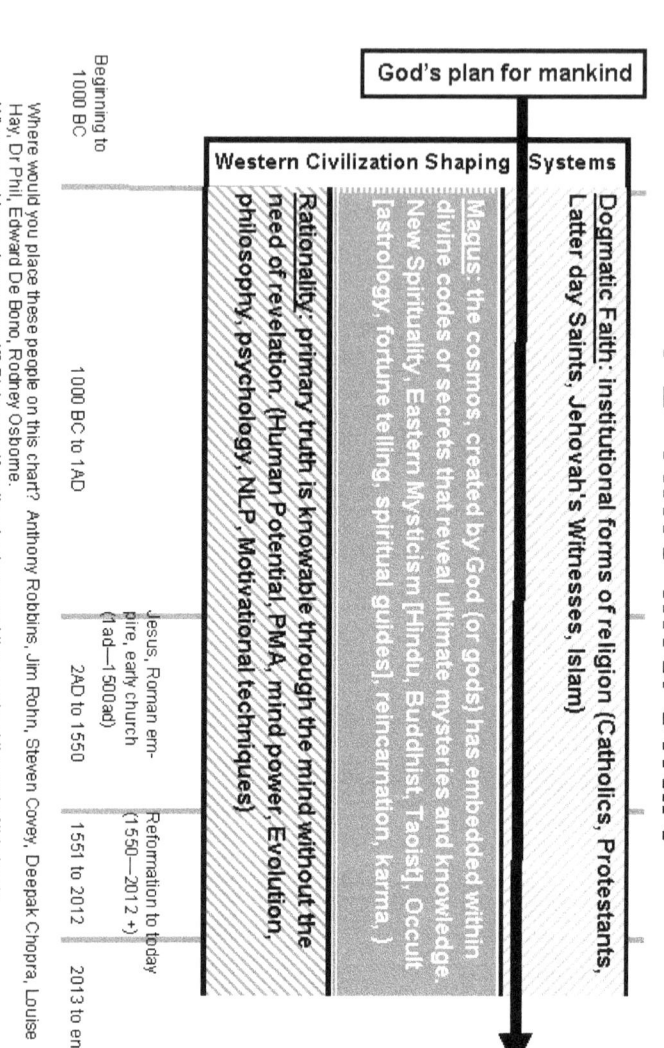

Has it changed? If so, why?

Conclusion

THIS BOOK HAS EXAMINED A BRIEF OUTLINE of the history of the Personal Development movement in an attempt to identify the source of all Personal Development, and this drive that humans have to better themselves. Mankind has been trying to live in unison with 'natural law' ever since he stepped out of synchronisation with it in that catastrophic event called the fall of man – when Adam, the first man, disobeyed God and ate the forbidden fruit.

Here lies the answer to why we are always trying to better ourselves. We want to get back to being who we were created to be, as Adam was in the Garden of Eden. Life was perfect there. Just an interesting observation here: an angel with a flaming sword was placed at the entrance to the garden to keep Adam from returning. If the garden represents the life that man as created for, the flaming sword represents the Word of God – the only thing that stands between man and the garden. Resist it and suffer the consequences. Adopt it, learn it, and believe it and eventually entrance back into the garden will be granted.

What we call 'natural law' is really God's law of creation. He created everything to work in harmony and it was, until man tipped the balance. Mankind has been working hard since then to regain that balance by developing the laws of Personal Development. But I fear a step has been missed.

> *"Physicists tend to believe that there are real laws to discover, but they find it difficult to answer questions about what they are and how they work."*[185]

---

[185] Jeff Stewart, *Why Balloons rise and apples fall* (London: Michael O'mara Books Limited, 2010). 21.

This book, The Parallax, has put forward what the Bible identifies as those fundamental laws as found in 2 Peter 1:5-7.

There is a 'hinge' in history that makes all the difference to this area of Personal Development. It is an event that the majority of Personal Development practitioners either don't know about, try to ignore, or just out-right reject. Yet it is the 'hinge' that makes all the difference. The difference between whether or not all the work done in Personal Development will be of any lasting value. That 'hinge' in history is the life, death, and resurrection of Jesus Christ.

Parallax: "the apparent displacement of an observed object due to a change in the position of the observer."

From the individual's parallax on this point, all the principles of Personal Development start to really make a difference.

> "8 the more you go on in this way (vs5-7), the more you will grow strong spiritually and become fruitful and useful to our Lord Jesus Christ. 9 but anyone who fails to go after these additions to faith is blind indeed, or at least very short-sighted, and has forgotten that God delivered him from the old life of sin so that now he can live a strong, good life for the Lord. 10 so, dear brothers, work hard to prove that you really are among those God has called and chosen, and then you will never stumble or fall away. 11 and God will open wide the gates of heaven for you to enter in to the eternal kingdom of our Lord and Saviour Jesus Christ."[186]

In summary this book has a message for three groups of people:

<u>The Believer who is committed:</u> to ongoing Personal Development will continually develop the principles outlined in 2 Timothy 1:5-7. They will grow strong, fruitful and useful

---

[186] Publishers, *Living Letters*: 310.II Peter 1:8-11

(Vs.8). Keep going and never forget that God plays the major role in your development.

<u>The believer who is not committed:</u> to Personal Development (Vs.9). Perhaps life has not gone as planned for you. There may be dreams and goals, long since abandoned and given up for dead and never to be accomplished. When this happens, one can often feel alone, as if they were the only one. But you are not. There have been many both in the past and right now, that also feel alone in the same lifestyle of failure. Look at how Mathews describes Moses:

> *"Moses was a man in whose heart a fire of zeal to accomplish God's great mission had burned fiercely forty years earlier. Now he is a man of lost vision, faded passion, and waning purpose…he had fled to the wilderness, his mission unaccomplished."*[187]

He stood Moses in front of a burning bush that was not consumed. The fire in Moses' belly had burned out because he was using his own fuel to try and keep it burning, but alas, he ran out of this kind of fuel. God showed Moses that there is another fire; a fire that will not burn out; a fire that requires no fuel to maintain its flame. It is the fire of the Holy Spirit that will bring our goals, dreams, vision, purpose and mission to accomplishment.

You must use 1 John 1:9 and be reinstated into full fellowship with God. This will fill you with the Holy Spirit and you will become the believer committed to ongoing Personal Development with the Bible as your primary source and first point of inquiry.

---

[187] R. Arthur Mathews, *Born for battle*, fourth ed. (England: Overseas Missionary Fellowship, 1978; repr., 1981). 98.

> *"12 I plan to keep on reminding you of these things...15 Hoping to impress them so clearly upon you that you will remember them long after I have gone."*[188]

It is to the non-believer: that this book has the most to say, even the most important and urgent of messages. By definition, the non-believer is without faith in Jesus Christ. Without a relationship with God, what has the non-believer got to better themselves through Personal Development? At a glance, there seems to be a great deal of Personal Development for them. There seems to be substantial growth generated with all the books, tapes, tools and 'new technologies' that are out there. As there is no inclusion of God, we have to put all the credit for this development under a title of 'human good'.

If you are a 'non-believer' and read the sections of this conclusion for believers, you may have noticed the word committed. The parallax between the believer and the non-believer is often in the commitment to a person, Jesus Christ, and the cause, Personal Development. A time in Japan serves as a good illustration of what happens when people are committed to a cause.

In the 15th and 16th century, the Japanese understood the idea of commitment to a cause. It was called 'Bushido:' the way of the warrior. They would sacrifice all, even life, without restraint or complaint for the 'cause.' So when 'Christianity' first came to the shores of Japan, via the Catholics, there was initially great success due to the already established concept of being committed to a cause. They readily did so with Christianity. Within 30 years there were 150,000 converts and 200 churches. Over the next 30 years, these figures doubled. Remember, these people were committed and have in history shown the strength of their commitment, but what is important is what or who the commitment is to. For the Japanese, it was to a cause. The result

---

[188] Publishers, *Living Letters*: 310.II Peter 1:12a, 15

was total failure. The church in Japan disintegrated and by 1640, these words were issued all over Japan:

> *"So long as the sun shall warm the earth let no Christian be so bold as to come to Japan; and let all know that the king of Spain himself, or the Christian's God, or the Great God of all, if he violate this command shall pay for it with his head."*[189]

This kept the church out of Japan for about 250 years (about 1890) The cause failed, and they always will eventually.

Before mankind can pat themselves on the back for the great achievements accomplished in the name of 'human good', or a cause and break out into a Elvis Presley impersonation singing 'I did it my way', take a look at what the Bible has to say about it. Human good is described as dead works.

> *"Therefore, having left the discourse of the beginning of Christ, let us go on to full growth, not laying again the foundation of repentance from dead works, and of faith toward God,"* (Heb 6:1)

God will not accept human good.

> *"But we are all as the unclean thing, and all our righteousnesses [human good works] are as a menstruation cloth. And we all fade as a leaf; and our iniquities, like the wind, have taken us away."* (Isa 64:6)

Human good won't place us in God's plan, nor does it have anything to do with it.

> *"who has saved us and called us with a holy calling, not according to our works, but according to His own purpose and grace which was given us in Christ Jesus before the eternal times."* (2Ti 1:9)

Human good will not save mankind.

---

[189] Young, *The Two Empires in Japan*: 20.

> *"not by works of righteousness which we have done, but according to His mercy He saved us, through the washing of regeneration and renewal of the Holy Spirit,"* (Tit 3:5)

All human good will be destroyed at the judgment seat of Christ.

> *"For any other foundation can no one lay than the one being laid, who is Jesus Christ. And if anyone builds on this foundation gold, silver, precious stones, wood, hay, stubble, each one's work shall be revealed. For the Day shall declare it, because it shall be revealed by fire; and the fire shall try each one's work as to what kind it is. If anyone's work which he built remains, he shall receive a reward. If anyone's work shall be burned up, he shall suffer loss. But he shall be saved, yet so as by fire. Do you not know that you are a temple of God, and that the Spirit of God dwells in you?"* (1Co 3:11-16)

Any good done by the non-believer or the carnal believer alike, is like the wood, hay, and stubble. It will be consumed by fire. Any good done by the believer is like the gold, silver, and precious stones. They will be refined by the fire. The 'good done' is the same. Here is the parallax. It is the 'position' of the person doing the good that makes the difference. It is the position of the believer, or that of the non-believer.

All human good will burned up with everything else on earth.

> *"But the day of the Lord will come as a thief in the night, in which the heavens will pass away with a rushing noise, and the elements will melt with fervent heat. And the earth and* **the works in it will be burned up.** *"* (2Pe 3:10)

The parallax is further seen in Titus 1:15-16:

> *"To the pure all things are pure. But to those who are defiled and unbelieving nothing is pure, but even their mind and conscience is defiled. They profess that they know God,* **but in their works** *they deny Him, being abominable and disobedient and reprobate* **to every good work.***"* (Tit 1:15-16)

This is how God looks upon 'human good':

> *"A right thing done in a wrong way – an antagonizing display of self-righteousness. God cannot abide this attitude."*[190]

There are several judgments mentioned in the Bible, and I want to draw attention to the one found in Revelations 20:11-12:

> *"And I saw a great white throne, and Him sitting on it, from whose face the earth and the heaven fled away. And a place was not found for them. And I saw the dead, the small and the great, stand before God. And books were opened, and another book was opened, which is the Book of Life. And the dead were judged out of those things which were written in the books, according to their works."* (Rev 20:11-12)

When most people hear this they think that those judged will be judged for their sins, however, there is no mention of sin at the great white throne. The judgment is 'according to their works'. Works, including human good, is the bases of the unbeliever's inditement at the last judgment.

All sin was and already has been dealt with through the blood of Christ at the cross. (1Jn.2:2)

> *"And if you call on the Father, who without respect of persons judges according to the work of each one, pass the time of your earthly residence in fear, knowing that*

---

[190] R. B. Thieme, *The Plan of God*: 12.

> *you were not redeemed with corruptible things, silver or gold, from your vain manner of life handed down from your fathers, **but with the precious blood of Christ**, as of a lamb without blemish and without spot;"* (1Pe 1:17-19)

> *"who does not need, as those high priests, to offer up sacrifice daily, first for his own sins and then for the people's sins. **For He did this once for all, when He offered up Himself.**"* (Heb 7:27)

Maintaining the position of being a non-believer rejects Christ and therefore cannot take advantage of what Christ has done for them in regards to the forgiveness of sin. The fact still remains; sin has been judged and cannot be judged again. We call that double jeopardy. The only thing to be judged is works. All works are recorded in that Book of Works.

What a shame, not to mention the waste, for a person to spend tens of thousands of dollars and incalculable amounts of energy working on Personal Development for the majority of their life, and adding to it good deeds, helping so many others, and being charitable, to find it is all for nothing!

It is all for nothing because the non-believers name is not in the other book: the Book of Life.

The Apostle Paul, previously known as Saul, found this out in time. He was highly educated and could be identified in today's terms as an expert in the field of Personal Development. Once he found Christ, look at what he had to say about all his Personal Development:

> *"But no, rather, I also count all things to be loss for the excellency of the knowledge of Christ Jesus my Lord, for whose sake **I have suffered the loss of all things, and count them to be dung, so that I may win Christ and be found in Him; not having my own righteousness,***

which is of the Law, but through the faith of Christ, the righteousness of God by faith," (Php 3:8-9)

Saul changed his name to Paul, because he experienced a change or shift in his position. He went from being a non-believer to being a believer. This is 'The Parallax.'

Will you change your position?

> *"Therefore also it is contained in the Scripture: "Behold, I lay in Zion a chief corner Stone, elect, precious, and he who believes on Him shall never be ashamed." Therefore to you who believe is the honor. But to those who are disobedient, He is the Stone which the builders rejected; this One came to be the Head of the corner, and a Stone-of-stumbling and a Rock-of-offense to those disobeying, who stumble at the Word, to which they also were appointed."* (1Pe 2:6-8)

Will Christ be the chief corner stone in your life (by believing on Him) or a constant stumbling block and a rock of offense (by rejecting Him)?

This decision, though small to say: simply believe on Him, is the biggest and most important of decisions. It makes all the difference to your Personal Development.

> *"...(for then He must have suffered often since the foundation of the world), but now once in the end of the world He has appeared to put away sin by the sacrifice of Himself."* (Heb 9:26)

> *"By this will we are sanctified through the offering of the body of Jesus Christ once for all. And indeed every priest stands daily ministering and offering often the same sacrifices, which can never take away sins. But this Man, after He had offered one sacrifice for sins forever, sat down on the right of God,"* (Heb 10:10-12)

Personal Development is God's idea and very much in His plan for your life.

> "God keeps you alive after salvation so that you can fulfil your personal destiny – to become a mature believer as an expression of God's glory in both time and eternity.... the quality and impact of your life on earth and your rewards in heaven depend on your execution of phase two."[191]

Notice that it is God's plan for you to fulfil your personal destiny. That is clear, but don't stop there. The reason you can fulfil your destiny is not a selfish or small one. It is to express God's glory here on earth, as well as in heaven.

If we go back to 1 Corinthians 3:11-13:

> "For any other foundation can no one lay than the one being laid, who is Jesus Christ. And if anyone builds on this foundation gold, silver, precious stones, wood, hay, stubble, each one's work shall be revealed. For the Day shall declare it, because it shall be revealed by fire; and the fire shall try each one's work as to what kind it is."

Like R. B. Theime, we can say, "...if you maintained your spiritual life...and advanced to spiritual maturity, your production is 'gold, silver, and precious stones.' Your Christian service qualifies as divine good and will not be consumed by fire."[192]

The parallax is more than being about Personal Development. It is about the advancement to spiritual maturity.

Here are a few final thoughts from the Bible and others to ponder:

---

[191] Ibid., 27.
[192] Ibid.

"The fool has said in his heart, There is no God! They acted corruptly; they have done abominable works, there is none who does good. Jehovah looked down from Heaven on the sons of men, to see if there were any who understood and sought God. All have gone aside, together they are filthy; there is none who does good, no, not one. Have all the workers of iniquity not known, eating up My people as they eat bread? They have not called on Jehovah. There they were in great fear; for God is in the generation of the righteous. You have shamed the counsel of the poor, because Jehovah is his refuge. Who will bring the salvation of Israel out of Zion? When Jehovah brings back the captivity of His people, Jacob shall rejoice, and Israel shall be glad." (Psa 14:1-7)

"The fool has said in his heart, There is no God. They acted corruptly, and have worked out abominable wickedness; there is not one doing good." (Psa 53:1)

"The lord works from the inside out. The world works from the outside in. The world would take people out of the slums. Christ takes the slums out of the people, and then they take themselves out of the slums. The world would mold men by changing their environment. Christ changes men, who then change their environment. The world would shape human behaviour, but Christ can change human nature." (Ezra Taft Benson)

"The moral fabric of society is disintegrating because we have thrown away the fear of the Lord and are trying to build on worldly, humanistic, secular philosophy".[193]

---

[193] Francis Wale Oke, *Victory in Spiritual Warfare* (London: Victory Literature Crusade, 1996).

> *"Satan's message is one of reformation and self-development rather than of regeneration."*[194]

Here is a final parallax. For some, this is a wonderful promise from God, should they be in the right position. For others, these same words are a warning, because of their position.

> *"and so that you might not say in your heart, My power and the might of my hand has gotten me this wealth. But you shall remember Jehovah your God, for it is He who gives you power to get wealth, so that He may confirm His covenant which He has sworn to your fathers, as it is today."* (Deu 8:17-18)

Which is it for you?

In closing: *"Beloved, do not believe every spirit, but try the spirits to see if they are of God, because many false prophets have gone out into the world."* (1Jn 4:1)

---

[194] Theodore H. Epp, *How to Resist Satan* (Nabraska: Back to the Bible, 1958).

The prayer to become a believer

The Bible says:

"He who believes on Him is not condemned, but he who does not believe is condemned already, because he has not believed in the name of the only-begotten Son of God." (Joh 3:18)

"He who believes on the Son has everlasting life, and he who does not believe the Son shall not see life, but the wrath of God abides upon him." (Joh 3:36)

When we say 'believe' we mean we personally believe that:

- Jesus Christ is the only begotten Son of God
- Jesus Christ came to die for your sins and provide everlasting life.

"And He [Jesus Christ] is the propitiation [atoning sacrifice] concerning our sins, and not concerning ours only, **but also concerning the sins of *all* the world."** (1Jn 2:2 , brackets mine)

To become a believer you must **personally believe** in the **Lord** Jesus Christ as your **Saviour.**

This is a very private matter that is between you and God. Tell Him now that you believe and are giving your life over to Him to be Lord of your life from this point forward.

If you haven't one already, start reading your Bible. The Gospel of John is a good place to start. I would be happy to send you a free copy of the Gospel if you don't have one. Just send me an email: kasumi.publishing@gmail.com with 'Gospel of John' as the subject. Don't forget to include your postal address so I can send it to you.

Appendix A - Doctrine of the five cycles of discipline

DOCTRINE OF THE FIVE CYCLES OF DISCIPLINE

R. B. Thieme, Jr. Bible Ministries | orig notes in 3/28/72; 6/14/76; 1/5/77; 10/28/79; 4/9/80 and others in 1991 | R. B. Thieme, Jr.

Posted on **Tuesday, 31 January 2006 3:12:34 PM** by **Cvengr**

The following Bible Class notes are provided on the topic in response to current events and debate from other perspectives.

These notes were from one Pastor-Teacher to his flock and congregation studying Scripture by his pastoring. Not all believers must follow this pastor, rather every believer has a responsibility to study Bible doctrine per the plan made for him by God in eternity past. For those reading these notes, not attending a church, you are encouraged to first come to belief in God through a very simple faith in Jesus Christ. If you have already had a saving faith, the issue is first to return to Him on His grounds by His methods by confessing your personal sins in prayer to the Father through faith in the Son. By 1st John 1:9, He is sure and just to forgive us our sins upon turning away from them and placing our faith in Him. Once this is done, and if interrupted, then repeated, returning to Him through faith in the Son, then continue to study per His guidance.

The Doctrine of the 5 Cycles of Discipline:

A. Background and Introduction.

1. The dispensation of Israel began with the Exodus in B.C. 1441 and concluded with the birth of our Lord in 4 B.C.

2. Therefore, most of the Old Testament Canon is devoted to the study of Jewish client nations. There were five Jewish client nations in the dispensation of Israel.

    a. The Theocratic Kingdom from the Exodus to the time of Samuel, B.C. 1441 - 1020.

    b. The United Kingdom from Saul to Rehoboam.,B.C.1020-926.

    c. The Northern Kingdom from Jeroboam to Hoshea, B.C.926-721. The fifth cycle of discipline was administered to the Northern Kingdom by Assyria, commanded by Sargon II.

d. The Southern Kingdom from Rehoboam to Zedekiah, B.C. 926 - 586. The fifth cycle of discipline was administered to the Southern Kingdom in 586 by the Chaldeans, commanded by Nebuchadnezzar. Seventy years of captivity or slavery extended from B.C. 586 - 516.

e. The restored nation of Judea from Zerubbabel in B.C. 536 - A.D. 70. The fifth cycle of discipline was administered to Judea by the Romans, first under the command of Vespasian and then by his son, Titus.

3. With the fall of Jerusalem in August of 70 A.D., there are no more Jewish client nations until the Second Advent.

4. In the meantime, we live in the times of the Gentiles. That means only a Gentile client nation can so function before God today.

5. At the present time, we the people of the United States are a Gentile client nation to God.

B. Definition of the Five Cycles of Discipline.

1. There are five cycles of discipline administered to a client nation, Jewish or Gentile.

   a. To the Jewish client nations during the dispensation of Israel, the dispensation of the Hypostatic Union, and the first forty years of the Church Age, the five cycles did function.

   b. To the Gentile client nations beginning with S.P.Q.R. in 70 A.D. and continuing to the present with the U.S.A., these five cycles are still operational.

2. Outline of the Five Cycles of Discipline.

   a. The first cycle of discipline, Lev 26:14-17.

   b. The second cycle of discipline, Lev 26:18-20.

   c. The third cycle of discipline, Lev 26:21-22.

   d. The fourth cycle of discipline, Lev 26:23-26.

   e. The fifth cycle of discipline, Lev 26:27-38, amplified in Deut 28:49-67.

3. The cycles of discipline are based on the principle that Jesus Christ controls history directly, indirectly, and permissively.

   a. He controls history directly through the function of His own divine essence.

b. He controls history indirectly through the function of the laws of divine establishment.

c. He controls history permissively through permitting nations to use their own volition to destroy themselves. For no nation is ever destroyed by an outside power before it is first destroyed from within by its own individual and collective bad decisions. Therefore, no nation is ever destroyed by another nation until it first destroys itself through negative volition.

4. Jesus Christ permits the policy of the angelic conflict (the function of free will) to continue and conclude in human history. Therefore, Satan's policy of good and evil must exist in every generation; there must be a challenge to your attitude toward doctrine.

5. Because Jesus Christ is righteous and holy, He must judge the nations with cycles of discipline.

6. These cycles of discipline are punitive measures against apostasy, reversionism and evil.

C. The First Cycle of Discipline, Lev 26:14-17.

1. Lev 26:14, "But if you do not obey Me and do not carry out all of these mandates,"

   a. Obedience in Israel meant the execution of God's plan for their dispensation. It meant the execution of the three categories of the Mosaic Law. It meant perception of doctrine as it was revealed at that time, first through the Torah and then through the prophets.

   b. The mandates refer to the three parts of the Mosaic Law. They are explained further in verse 15.

2. Lev 26:15, "If instead you reject My statutes and your soul despises My ordinances, and you fail to carry out all my commands so breaking My covenant," The Mosaic Law is divided into three parts.

   a. The first part of the Mosaic Law is the decalogue, the freedom code made up of ten commandments. These commandments define freedom in terms of morality, privacy, property, and authority. Freedom without authority is anarchy; authority without freedom is tyranny. The ten commandments also define freedom in terms of relationship with God.

   b. The second part is called the ordinances, the spiritual code. It graphically presents soteriology and Christology through the various articles of furniture in the Tabernacle and temples, through the modus operandi of the levitical priesthood, through the function of the holy days, and through the levitical sacrifices. This spiritual code presents the Gospel and Jesus Christ as the God of Israel.

c. The third part is the judgments, an establishment code. It includes explanations related to freedom, privacy, marriage, criminal law, taxation (tithing), military policy and freedom through military victory, diet, health, sanitation, quarantine, free enterprise, and profit motivation. It outlaws violence, terrorism, civil disobedience, and revolution.

3. Lev 26:16, "Then I will do this to you: I will bring upon you sudden terror [terrorism], epidemic diseases, and fever will destroy your sight and drain your life; also, you will plant your seed in vain because your enemies will devour it."

a. "Sudden terror" is the function of terrorism as it existed in the ancient world. It is also a reference to violence, unrestrained criminality, and hostility from other nations.

b. Many epidemics have been the beginning of the end of great nations or empires.

c. The last phrase refers to economic disaster and depression. The illustration used refers to an agricultural economy. In our industrial economy, this refers to inability to compete with foreign markets.

4. Lev 26:17, "I will set My face against you so that you will be defeated by your enemies; consequently, those who hate you will rule over you, and you will flee when no one is pursuing you."

a. In the first cycle, such defeat by enemies refers to only preliminary wars. But before the other cycles of discipline are administered, there is already loss in warfare. (Our loss in warfare began with Korea and Vietnam.)

b The Hebrew word for hate here means hate based on envy. The Jews were the recipients of such fantastic blessings from God that they were envied and then hated.

c. "You will flee when no one is pursuing you" is an idiom saying that the general population becomes cowardly, afraid of war. They have no motivation from patriotism or the spiritual life. Therefore, the population will do anything to avoid a war, even surrendering whatever advantage it has in national and international activity.

D. The Second Cycle of Discipline, Lev 26:18-20.

1. Lev 26:18, "If after all these things you will not listen to Me, then I will punish you on an intensified basis seven more times for your sins."

a. The first phrase implies that some wake up as a result of the first cycle of discipline.

b. Everything in the first cycle is intensified in the second cycle by seven.

2. Lev 26:19, "Then I will also break down [destroy] the arrogance of your power; I will make your sky like iron and your earth like bronze."

a. Notice that once the first cycle of discipline is administered and it does not turn around the nation, arrogance sets in. Arrogance is a whole complex of sins and evil.

b. Today we have the greatest arrogance in places of power. God actually punishes such arrogance among those in power without the humility to use their power properly.

c. The sky like iron and the earth like bronze refers to a drought. Drought means economic disaster, resulting in economic depression.

3. Lev 26:20, "Then your strength will be spent uselessly, for your land will not yield its produce, nor will the trees of the land bear their fruit."

a. No matter how hard you work, you cannot produce food.

b. The Bible should be interpreted in the time in which it was written. This was written in during an agricultural economy before the industrial revolution.

4. So the second cycle of discipline is a depression, bad social life, no national pride, and people work hard for nothing (inflation).

E. Third Cycle of Discipline, Lev 26:21-22.

1. Lev 26:21, "If therefore you remain hostile to Me [negative volition toward Bible doctrine], and you are not willing to hear Me, I will multiply your epidemics seven times more as your sins deserve."

a. God did not speak directly to them but indirectly through His communicators, which at that time were the prophets.

b. In the third cycle, there is the intensification of epidemics and illnesses in the land. In our day, AIDs will break this country if the trend continues, for it is a very serious problem, and may rival the bubonic plague of the Middle Ages.

2. Lev 26:22, "I will send wild animals [criminals] against you and they will rob you of your children; they will destroy your cattle and so reduce your population that your roads will be deserted." With the end of civilization, violence overflows from both animals and people.

3. In the third cycle, the population is thinned out by violence. Crime gets out of control; commerce is stopped; there are natural disasters.

F. The Fourth Cycle of Discipline, Lev 26:23-26.

1. So far nothing but grace warnings have been given. Now God will really judge the nation. There will be great uncontrollable crime, military invasion and partial defeat, disease from overcrowding, a shortage of food causing starvation, and even greater natural disasters. Examples can be found by studying Israel in 68 A.D., 586 B.C., and 721 B.C.

2. Lev 26:23, "And if by these things you will not be corrected by Me, but will continue to be hostile toward Me [negative volition from cosmic involvement in the stages of reversionism],"

3. Lev 26:24, "Then I will go into opposition toward you [literally: act with hostility toward you], and I will strike you seven times more for your sins." Again, there is the intensification of the characteristics of all the cycles, with something more added, as stated in verse 25.

4. Lev 26:25, "I will bring the sword upon you to avenge the breaking of the covenant, and when you retreat into your cities I will send a plague [epidemic] among you, so that you will be delivered into the hands of your enemies."

> a. One of the great signs of loss of freedom, and replacing it with both moral and immoral degeneracy, is when you see the breakdown of the military establishment. The entire book of Numbers is devoted to setting up a mobilization plan for the military.
>
> b. The part of the covenant that was broken was the military part. There was military disaster as a result. Why did the Jews have to retreat into their cities? Because their cities were fortified, and their armies could not win in the field. Once there are overcrowded cities, disease becomes rampant (as illustrated by the Romans when fleeing from Hannibal).

5. Lev 26:26, "When I cut off your food supply, ten women will bake your bread in one oven, and they will dole out your bread by weight, so that you will eat and never be satisfied."

> a. When an army begins to lose a war on its own soil, the first thing to go is food supply. People start to starve, as the south did in the last year of the War between the States. So one of the inevitable results of the fourth cycle of discipline is the beginning of starvation.

b. Ten women baking bread in one oven means there is food rationing. Therefore, after eating a small piece of bread, you are just as hungry as you were before, and even more so.

G. The Fifth Cycle of Discipline, Lev 26:27-38.

1. Now there is nothing to eat. Enemies have taken over the country. People are put into slavery. People are afraid of everything. Everyone has become a coward.

2. Lev 26:27, "If, in spite of this, you do not listen to Me but continue to be hostile toward Me [toward the message of Bible doctrine]," The only hope is Bible doctrine; there is no hope beyond Bible doctrine. The only hope for the nation is found in believers.

3. Lev 26:28, "Then in My anger I will be hostile toward you [no more grace], and I will punish you seven times more for your sins."

4. Lev 26:29, "Then you will eat the flesh of your sons, and you will eat the flesh of your daughters."

> a. No longer do you eat bread and rationed food, as in the fourth cycle; now you eat people! Cannibalism is the total malfunction of all establishment principles. One of the strongest of all establishment principles is the family and the love of parents for children. But in those days, parents will eat their children.

> b. This type of cannibalism actually occurred between 66 and 70 A.D. among Jews under the seige of Jerusalem by the Roman army. Josephus documented such things. Civilization suddenly departs in the fifth cycle of discipline.

5. Lev 26:30, "Then I will destroy your high places and cut down your incense altars, and stack your corpses on the dumb corpses of your idols, for My soul will despise you." The high places are the meeting places of false doctrine and cults, especially the phallic cult.

6. Lev 26:31, "I will turn your cities into ruins, and lay waste to your sanctuaries; I will take no delight in the fact that you suddenly start offering sacrifices."

7. Lev 26:32-33, "I will make the land desolate so that your enemies will settle in it, and will be appalled by its condition. You, however, I will scatter among the nations, and I will draw out My sword and pursue you, and your cities will lie in ruins."

a. The territory is occupied.

b. Being scattered among nations means you go into slavery. This happened three times to the Jewish people.

8. Lev 26:34, "Then the land will satisfy its Sabbaths . . . , while you are in the land of your enemies; consequently, the land will rest and be paid its Sabbaths." The Jews had ignored seventy Sabbatical years, and therefore the Southern Kingdom had seventy years under slavery.

9. Lev 26:35, "All the days of its desolation [fifth cycle] it will observe the rest which it did not observe in your sabbatical years while you were living in the land."

10. Lev 26:36, "As for those of you who survive [the fifth cycle], I will make their right lobes so afraid in the lands of their enemies that the sound of a wind-blown leaf will put them into flight. In fact, when no one is pursuing, they will run as though fleeing from an army, and they will fall even when no one is pursuing." People do die of fright.

11. Lev 26:37, "Furthermore, they will fall over each other as if fleeing from the sword, although no one is pursuing them; consequently, you will have no strength." No strength means no military establishment for freedom, and no patriotic motivation. It's too late in the fifth cycle of discipline, because it takes a long time to train a military establishment.

12. Lev 26:38, "But you will perish among the nations, and the land of your enemies will devour you." Enemies of the Jews were those like Assyria, Chaldea, and Rome.

13. Deut 28:49-67 is another horrible description of the fifth cycle of discipline.

14. Isaiah warned the Northern Kingdom and Jeremiah warned the Southern Kingdom during the first administration of the fifth cycle of discipline to each of these nations.

H. Historical Examples of the Administration of the Fifth Cycle of Discipline to Jewish Client Nations.

1. The fifth cycle of discipline was administered to Assyria, Ezek 31:3-14.

2. The fifth cycle of discipline was administered to the Northern Kingdom, Hos 4:1-6, in 721 B.C. Elijah, Elisha, Amos and Hosea all prophesied the coming of the fifth cycle of discipline. 2 Kgs 17 gives the historical account. Isa 28:1-13 gives the prophetical account.

3. The fifth cycle of discipline was administered to the Southern Kingdom in 586 B.C., Jer 50:17, 7:24-29, because they did not listen to the teaching of doctrine, Jer 15:5-6, 13:10-11,17, 17:27, 35:13.

    a. The overt manifestation of Jewish reversionism in the Southern Kingdom was idolatry, Jer 2:27-30, 3:9, 7:17-20, 13:10,17:1-4.

    b. The duration of the first fifth cycle of discipline to the Southern Kingdom was seventy years, all of their sabbatical years. Cf Ex 23:10-11;Lev 25:3-4, 26:33-36;2 Chr 36:20-21;Jer 25:11-12, 29:10; Dan 9:2, 24-27.

4. The fifth cycle of discipline was administered to Judea in 70 A.D.

    a. This was prophesied by our Lord in Lk 21:20-24.

    b. They were also warned by the teaching of Paul. The gift of tongues was also a warning to Israel that they were about to lose their status as a priest nation to God.

    c. The dispensation of the Church and the completion of the Jewish Age both occur while Israel is out under the fifth cycle of discipline.

5. Grace always precedes the fifth cycle of discipline by the warnings of the first four cycles. In the fifth cycle of discipline, you either are killed or become enslaved.

I. The Fifth Cycle of Discipline to the Northern Kingdom.

1. The Northern Kingdom was established as a result of a revolution, based on jealousy of Judah, the Southern Kingdom, 1 Chr 12:30; Ps 60:7; 2 Sam 19:40-43.

2. Mental attitude sins like jealousy destroy capacity for love. The Northern Kingdom never had the basis to love God because it was founded on jealousy. A kingdom founded on emotional revolt of the soul will inevitably destroy itself. Being built up by emotional revolt, the actual incident that kicked off the revolution was human good when the people complained to Rehoboam with their grievance.

3. The Northern Kingdom began with Jeroboam in 926 B.C. He was in emotional revolt of the soul.

4. Even though the Northern Kingdom had such a bad start, God in His grace tried to stabilize the Northern Kingdom. God provided for the Northern Kingdom special prophets who warned the Northern Kingdom against apostasy and tried to communicate to them the principles of freedom. Four outstanding prophets were involved in this grace push by our Lord.

a. Elijah, c.871-851 B.C.

b. Elisha, c.845 B.C..

c. Amos, 787 B.C.

d. Hosea, c. 746 B.C.

5. Amos warned the Northern Kingdom in 787 B.C. during the reign of Jeroboam II. Hosea warned the Northern Kingdom, c.746 B.C., during the fourth cycle of discipline when Tiglath-PileserIII was the Assyrian king. In addition, Isaiah provided some warning, as in the first part of Isa 28.

6. The fifth cycle of discipline is described in two passages of the Old Testament, so that both the Northern Kingdom and Southern Kingdom had adequate warning about it; Lev 26:27-46; Deut 28:49-67.

7. The historical account of the fifth cycle of discipline to the Northern Kingdom is found in 2 Kg 17:1-12.

8. The prophetical account of the fifth cycle of discipline to the Northern Kingdom is found in Isa 28:1-13 and mentioned in Jer 3:8.

9. Before judgment came to the Northern Kingdom, and during the two years in which the Assyrians were in the Northern Kingdom and even afterward, Jews of the Northern Kingdom fled to the Southern Kingdom and became citizens there, 1 Chr 9:3.

10. Therefore, there is no such thing as the "ten lost tribes." The ten tribes of the Northern Kingdom, from the time of Elijah down to the time when Shalmanezer invaded, constantly fled south. So all the tribes were represented in the Southern Kingdom after the Northern Kingdom fell.

11. The fifth cycle of discipline began in 721 B.C. with the fall of Samaria. The Assyrians' seige began under Shalmanezer V (who died), and ended when Sargon II defeated the Northern Kingdom in battle, Jer 50:17a.

J. The Fifth Cycle of Discipline to the Southern Kingdom.

1. Deut 28:49-67 was fulfilled.

2. The first administration to the Southern Kingdom of the fifth cycle of discipline is called the Babylonian captivity, Jer 50:17b. The time was 586 B.C. The administrator was the Chaldean Empire under Nebuchadnezzar.

3. The second administration to the Southern Kingdom is the present dispersion, Lk 21:40-25. Its time period is August 70 A.D. to the Second Advent. Its administrator was Rome under Vespasian and Titus.

4. The reason for the fifth cycle of discipline was the rejection of Bible doctrine, Jer 7:24-29, 13:10,11,17, 15:5-6, 17:27, 35:13.

5. The overt cause of the fifth cycle of discipline was apostasy and idolatry (which resulted in rejection of Bible doctrine), Jer 2:27-30, 3:9, 7:17-20, 13:10, 17:1-4.

6. The length of the first administration of the fifth cycle of discipline was seventy years. This was determined on the basis of the Jews having rejected seven Sabbatical years over a period of 490 years, Jer 25:11-12, 29:10; Dan 9:2,24-27.

7. During the present dispersion, there are two substitutes for the nation Israel.

    a. The Church Age, where every believer is a priest.

    b. The Tribulation, when 144,000 Jews represent the Lord, Rev 7 and 14.

K. Why the cycles of discipline to client nations? Hosea 4:1-6.

1. This passage is addressed to believers. For in the final analysis, it is the believers who are responsible for the rise or fall of a client nation.

2. Hos 4:1, "Hear the word of the Lord, you citizens of Israel [Northern Kingdom] because the Lord has a case [indictment] against the inhabitants of the client nation, because nothing of doctrine is taught, nothing about grace is being applied; there is no knowledge of God in the land."

    a. Just as God had an indictment against the Jewish client nations, so today He has an indictment against a Gentile client nation, the United States of America.

    b. "Because nothing of doctrine is taught." There is no demand for Bible teaching in time of apostasy.

    c. As a result, "nothing of grace is being applied." Grace and doctrine go together. When they are both gone, that is one of the reasons for the five cycles of discipline.

3. Hos 4:2, "Instead, there is lying [dishonesty], deception, homicide, stealing, rape, therefore blood touches blood [idiom for perpetual violence]."

4. Hos 4:3, "Therefore, the land mourns, and all who live in it languish along with the beasts of the field and the birds of the air."

    a. "The land mourns" means the people are miserable under the cycles of discipline. No one is enjoying anything or having any fun. Social life, business life, and spiritual life are gone; there is nothing but abject misery.

b. "All who live in it languish" means loss of national courage, patriotism, vitality, and strength.

c. Animals suffer when people suffer. People are viciously cruel under the cycles of discipline.

5. Hos 4:4, "Yet let no one find fault [as in evil activism]; let no one offer criticism, for your citizens are like those who contend with the priests [communicators of doctrine]."

a. Activism is the last thing you need to get into when under the cycles of discipline.

b. Criticism is blaming other groups. It is the believer who must take the responsibility for these things himself. It is negative volition and a shrinking pivot that brings these things.

6. Hos 4:5, "Therefore, you have stumbled in the daylight, and even the prophet will stumble with you in the night darkness; and I will destroy your native country [motherland]."

a. Stumbling in the daylight means cosmic involvement, including crusader arrogance. Daylight means becoming a loser by rejecting Bible doctrine after hearing it, or failing to metabolize gnosis doctrine into epignosis doctrine.

b. "And even the prophet will stumble with you" means prophets become false prophets and they teach false doctrine.

c. Today, hundreds of thousands of pulpits speak of "`peace, peace,' when there is no peace," just as they said in Jeremiah's day, Jer 6:14, 8:11; Ezek 13:10, 16. Today, pastors peddle false doctrine while the United States is declining for lack of pivot.

d. There can be no pivot without the pastor-teacher communicating the mystery doctrine for the Church Age. There can be no pivot without the manufacture of invisible heroes.

7. Hos 4:6, "My people are destroyed by lack of knowledge of doctrine. Because you have rejected the knowledge of doctrine, I will reject you from being My priest nation."

a. A client nation to God is a priest nation in that it represents God under three factors. The freedom developed in the client nation means:

(1) Freedom for evangelism in the nation.

(2) Freedom to teach doctrine in the nation.

(3) Freedom to send missionaries to other countries to communicate the Gospel, and form the converts into indigenous local churches.

b. Today, the United States is a priest nation. It may not be tomorrow. The only hope for this country resides in your soul. If there is negative volition, we will go down. If there is a surge in positive volition, it could form a large enough pivot to deliver this country.

c. A nation without Bible doctrine is a nation without solutions.

d. As goes the believer, so goes the client nation to God.

8. This prophecy given in Hosea 4 was fulfilled to the Northern Kingdom. What happened to greater nations than we in the past can certainly happen to us tomorrow.

R. B. Thieme, Jr. Bible Ministries
5139 West Alabama, Houston, Texas 77056, (713) 621-3740
(c) 1991, by R. B. Thieme, Jr. All rights reserved.

Bibliography

Bainton, Ronald H. *A History of Christianity*. London: Thomas Nelson & Sons, 1964.
Barnhouse, Donald Grey. *The Invisable War*. Grand Rapids, Michigan: Zondervan Publishing House, 1965.
Boer, Harry R. In *A short History of the Early Church,* edited Grand Rapids, Michigan: William B. eerdmans, 1976.
Bono, Edward de. *Teach Your Child How to Think*. London: Penguin Books, 1992.
Branon, Dave. "The Debt of Leadership." *Our daily Bread*, no. March, April, May 2008 (2008).
———. "A Place to Stand." *Our daily Bread* June July August (2008).
Cetas, Anne. "Fever Pitch." *Our daily Bread* December January February (2009).
———. "Serving Together." *Our daily Bread*, no. June, July, August 2008 (2008).
Collins, Jim. *Good to Great*. New York: HarperCollins House, 2001.
Covey, Stephen R. *The 8th Habit*. New York: Free Press, 2004.
Covey, Stephen R. *The 7 Habits of Highly Effective People*. 2004.
Crowder, Bill. "Looking Ahead." *Our daily Bread* June July August (2011).
———. "The Richness of Humility." *Our daily Bread*, no. March, April, May 2008 (2008).
———. "The Search for Justice." *Our Daily Bread*, no. June, July, August 2008 (2008).
———. "Too Soon to Quit." *Our daily Bread* June July August (2007).
Dallas Willard, Don Simpson. *Revolution of Character*. Nottingham: Inter-Varsity Press, 2006.
Dictionary. 2010.
Dr. Henry Cloud, Dr John Townsend. *How People Grow*. Sydney: Strand Publishing, 2001.
Drane, John. *Introducing the New Testament*. third ed. Oxford: A Lion Book, 2010.
"Endures." *Our daily Bread*, no. 2008 (2008).
Epp, Theodore H. *How to Resist Satan*. Nabraska: Back to the Bible, 1958.
Fisher, Dennis. "What Are You Known For?". *Our daily Bread*, no. June, July, August 2011 (27/6/2011 2011).
Funahashi, Yoichi. "March 11 - Japan's Zero Hour." *Time*, July 8 2011 2011.
Girard, Chuck. "Don't Shoot the Wounded." In *Name above all names*: Sea of Glass Music, 1982.
Gonzalez, Justo L. *The Story of Christianity*. The Early Church to the Dawn of the Reformation. Vol. 1, New York: Harper Collins, 2010.

———. *The Story of Christianity, Volume 2, the Reformation to the Present Day*. Vol. 2, New York: HarperCollins, 2010.
Haan, D. De. "Building a City." *Our daily Bread* September October November (2008).
Haun, Mart de. "Urge to Jump." *Our daily Bread* March April May (2008).
Henry, Matthew. *Matthew Henry's Commentary on the Whole Bible*. London: Marshall Morgan & Scott, 1960.
Hia, C. P. "Building a City." *Our daily Bread* September October November (2008).
House, Zondervan Publishing. *The Amplified Bible*. Grand Rapids, Michigan: Zondervan Publishing House, 1987.
Inglis, James. *Fighting Talk*. Millers Point: Murdoch Books Australia, 2008.
Jim Collins, Jerry I. Porras. *Built to Last*. New York: HarperCollins House, 1994.
Latourette. *A History of Christianity*. Harper, 1975.
Link, Julie Ackerman. "Bribery." *Our daily Bread*, no. June, July, August 2010 (27 July 2010).
———. "Celebrate Freedom." *Our daily Bread*, no. June, July, August 2007 (2007).
———. "Chimp Eden." *Our Daily Bread*, no. June, July, August 2009 (2009).
———. "Failure to Discipline." *Our daily Bread*, no. June July August (2011).
———. "Poetic Justice." *Our daily Bread*, no. September, October, November 2011 (2011).
———. "Strength in Weakness." *Our daily Bread*, no. December, January, Febuary 2009-2010 (2010).
Man, The Spiritual. *Watchman Nee*. 1977.
Mathews, R. Arthur. *Born for Battle*. fourth ed. England: Overseas Missionary Fellowship, 1978. 1981. 1978.
Maxwell, John C. *Talent Is Never Enough*. Nashville: Thomas Nelson, 2007.
McCasland, David. "The Next Generation." *Our daily Bread*, no. March April May (2008).
———. "Running Every Day." *Our daily Bread* June July August (2009).
McCullough, Christopher J. *Nobodies Victim*. New York: Clarkson Potter/Publishers, 1995.
McGraw, Dr Phillip c. *Life Strategies*. United Kingdom: Vermillion, 1999.
E-Sword Version 10.0.5.
Nee, Watchman. *The Spiritual Man*. 1977.
Oke, Francis Wale. *Victory in Spiritual Warfare*. London: Victory Literature Crusade, 1996.

Our Daily Bread. RBC, 2011.
Packer, James I. "Why We Need the Puritans." (1996): 9-13.
Pink, Arthur W. *Practical Christianity*. sixth, 1990 ed. Grand Rapids, Michigan: Baker Book House, 1974.
Porras, Jim Collins & Jerry I. *Built to Last*. 1997.
Publishers, Tyndale House. *Living Letters*. Wheaton, Illinois: Tyndale House Publishers, 1962. Paraphrase.
R. B. Thieme, Jr. *445-0001*. texas: R. B. Thieme, Jr., Bible Ministries, 1972.
———. "445-0005." 1972.
———. "Better Things for Christmas." Houston, Texas: R. B. Thieme, Jr., Bible Ministries, 2003.
———. *Christian Integrity*. Houston Texas: R. B. Thieme Jr. Bible Ministries, 2002, 1997, 1984.
———. *The Faith-Rest Life*. Texas: R. B. Thieme Jr. Bible Ministries, 2004, 1999, 1961.
———. *The Plan of God*. Texas: R. B. Thieme Jr., Bible Ministries, 1972, 1973, 1992, 2003.
———. *The Trinity*. Texas: R. B. Thieme Jr., Bible Ministries, 1972, 1975, 1993, 2003.
R. B. Thieme, Jr. *Freedom through Military Victory*. Texas: R. B. Thieme, JR, 2003.
Richards, Lawrence O. *The Daily Devotional Commentary*. USA: Victor Books, 1990.
Senge, Peter M. *The Fifth Discipline*. Australia: Random House, 1990.
Shelley, Bruce L. *Church History in Plain English*. Thomas Nelson, 1975.
Simpson, Dallas Willard & Don. *Revolution of Character*. Nottingham: Inter-Varsity Press, 2006.
Stewart, Jeff. *Why Balloons Rise and Apples Fall*. London: Michael O'mara Books Limited, 2010.
Stowell, Joe. "Small Things." *Our daily Bread*, no. March April May (2011).
———. "The Song of the Saints." *Our Daily bread*, no. June, July, August 2009 (2009).
———. "When Life Seems Unfair." *Our daily Bread*, no. March, April, May 2011 (2011).
Stowell, Joseph M. *Eternity: Reclaiming a Passion for What Endures*. Grand Rapids: Discovery House Publishers, 2006.
Tillich, Paul. *A History of Christian Thought*. New York: A Touchstone Book, Simon and Schuster, 1967, 1968.
V. Raymond Edman, Ph.D., LL.D. *The Disciplines of Life*. Illinois: Scripture Press, 1948. eight.
Vaughan, Curtis. *The New Testament from 26 Translations*. Grand Rapids, Michigan: Zondervan Publishing House, 1967, 1977.

"Wikipedia." 2011.
Williams, Marvin. "One Passion." *Our daily Bread* June July August (2009).
Young, John M. L. *The Two Empires in Japan.* Tokyo: The Bible Times Press, 1958.

Other publications
But, He was with me & Australian Adventure

Strangers and Aliens

Available from: **www.kasumigundan.com**
Subscribe to Rodney's Blog: **rodneyjosborne.wordpress.com**
Feedback: Please email any feedback or comments on this book on:
kasumi.publishing@gmail.com

www.ingramcontent.com/pod-product-compliance
Lightning Source LLC
Chambersburg PA
CBHW071420160426
43195CB00013B/1757